Release the Dove
By Rhonda Wilson-Dikoko

Foreword

This is a powerful testimony of a grandmother's unconditional love for her grandson and undaunted faith in our Almighty God, where trust, hope and perseverance lead to his miracle healing. Many parallels can be found in this epic life story and many lessons to learn from it; as the love which Rhonda bestows on her grandson depicts God's love for us.

Rhonda crossed my path in Kuala Lumpur where I got to know this strong willed woman, passionate for the works of God. In everything she does honor and glory belong to God alone, her heavenly voice sounding praises to His Kingdom from the very first moment you meet her. In this journey with her grandson you will encounter how her faith, belief and trust in God through difficult encounters lead to her grandson's healing.

Rhonda has been in ministry most of her adult life; she was ordained into the ministry of Double Portion Church in September 2001 where Pastor Hayes Moss is the Senior Pastor. Prior to that, she was sent out from the Double Portion Church as a Missionary in 1988. She travelled with the Assistant Pastor, Sarah Banks, as her Interpreter in Congo, Gabon, France, Holland and Rwanda. In Congo she served on the ministerial team of Nazareth Church from 1989 to 1997 in the capacity of Evangelist and she and her husband were in charge of the Married Group Ministry. Nazareth Church started an orphanage whereby she was the director. In Gabon, from 1998 to 2001, she served on the Bethany Ministry Team as Evangelist and conducted Bible Explorers for children. In Nigeria she hosted Hannah's Fellowship, a woman's Bible study from 2002 to 2005. She also ran a Bible Explorer's Club for children. During the period 2007 to 2009 she served in Shepherds Place Ministry as Choir Director and Youth Leader in Holland. In Malaysia she served at The Ambassadors International Church as Evangelist, as well as the Married Group Leader with her husband from 2010 until 2015. She was also the Leader of Oasis Women's Bible Study from 2009 up to 2015.

Elmine Knight

1 Corinthians 2:5 (NIV), "So that your faith might not rest on human wisdom, but on God's power."

Dedication

This book is dedicated to Pastor Moss and Sister Banks of the Double Portion Church - for their years of supporting my Missionary Outreach.

To Reverend Amos Great- my Pastor in Kuala Lumpur- thanks for your love and support to my family over the years.

To Oasis Bible Study who believed in me as their leader for 5+ years and urged me to tell this story.

To Carol Smart my walking buddy who rallied the ladies to pray, I will forever be grateful.

To Barb Angell who worked behind the scenes to facilitate my exodus from KL, to Loma, who accepted to step in my shoes, to all the leading ladies and Oasis Family – You're simply the Best!

To Alesea and Mel who entrusted their son to our care.

To Dorothy Chemezie– my Spiritual daughter who called relentlessly and prayed fervently for a miracle! You rock!

To Obiale and Danielle, the "grown up kids" as my grand-son has always referred to them.

To all those who prayed and wept with us who visited us at hospital and encouraged others to pray. Prayer is so essential. Without it I would not have felt such peace in the midst of my storm. Many thanks and much love!

To all the doctors and nurses who cared for our grand-son.

A tribute goes to my deceased Father, Archie Wilson Sr. who insured that all of his children were in Church every time the door opened! I appreciate you so much Daddy! You would be amazed how your words of wisdom and advice have followed me and my siblings all our lives.

To my Lord and King – My rock, my fortress, my ever present help in time of need, The I am that I am, Ancient of Days, Balm in Gilead, Jehovah Rophe, True and faithful, The One who is and is to come. I worship you and count it grace to be numbered amongst your chosen.

In His Service,

Rhonda Wilson-Dikoko (aka Koko)

I wrote this poem when Olivier was born, August 3, 2005

Infinity Love

So tiny and so precious and beautiful is he,
Who would ever believe?
That this angel was sent to me.

You came much too soon,
We were totally caught by surprise.
Yet when you appeared into our world on August 3rd,
All the pain & fears we had all disappeared.

I love you more than anything,
And I will always pray
That the Lord would grant you peace.
And in His perfect will you would stay.

I pray that the Lord would guide and protect you
And keep you through the storms of life.
Help you when you stumble,
Keep you away from strife.

So just how much do you love me Koko?
I'm sure one day you may ask.
Infinity x2,   forever and always!

By Rhonda Wilson-Dikoko

Prelude

Walking into Pastor Moss's office in February 2016 after many months of not seeing him made me appreciate he and the Double Portion Church even more. It was there that I had been baptized, married and inducted into the fivefold Ministry. Pastor Moss represented stability and an unshakable faith and an unquenchable desire to know Christ more! Even at his ripe old age, he still spent time in fasting and seeking God. His ministry spanned over 60 years of preaching, teaching, writing books and doing radio ministry.

My Pastor is a man of faith, believing in divine healing and has memorized the entire Bible by heart. He has always preached the undisputed Word of God and stressed the importance of speaking the Word. I hold him in very high esteem. When he saw me a few days before my birthday in February 2016, he started speaking the Word over my life and prophesying,

"God's got your back, Sister Rhonda," he said. "Where ever you go, Release the Dove. It takes three things to live a life of faith: Righteousness, faith and grace. ***God is able to make all grace abound toward you, always having sufficiency in all things; you may have abundance for every good work.***

2 Corinthians 9:8 NKJV

*"**For the law of the Spirit of life has set you free in Christ Jesus from the law of sin and death.**" Romans 8:2"*

I had related to him my testimony regarding my grandson the year before but I'm not certain whether he remembered my grand-son's name and certainly he did not know the circumstances around his illness.

When Pastor Moss commanded me to "Release the Dove" everywhere I go, the words resounded in my spirit. I knew there would be a revelation to come and I was expectant to know just what it was.

A few days later the Holy Spirit shed some more light on this revelation. Perusing antique shops is one of my favorite past-times. I happened to have been in my home-town in Fayette, Alabama on my birthday! This was the first time in years that I had been home to celebrate! Memories of birthdays past spun through my mind. My Mother had always made my birthday so special even if in simplicity. I chose to take a long walk and breathe in the fresh crisp country air. Then I drove into town and wandered into an antique shop before driving to my daughter's in Huntsville, Alabama.

I found a perfect picture frame for my grand-daughter and purchased it. While waiting for my receipt, I caught a glimpse of something white out of the corner of my eye. I turn to give my full attention to this magnificent find. There in an inconspicuous spot in that overcrowded antique shop sat a pair of doves!

'How much are those?' I asked the shop keeper unable to contain my excitement. 'It says $20 on the bottom if I can get both, I'll take them.' I said in a raspy voice.

'Sold,' he replied, taking the doves out of my hands and wrapping them carefully in paper. How unique to have found two doves in this antique shop on my birthday! A double portion blessing indeed!

My Pastor is not a man of many words. But when he speaks, you better believe it is prolific!

Marrying my Congolese husband in my picturesque quaint white steeple church nearly 30 years ago, Pastor Moss pronounced words over our marriage that would change the course of our history together. He spoke these words, "Lord tie them up tight, and bind them together, nothing separating."

The Bible says in Ecclesiastes 4:12b NLT, **"Three are even better, for a triple-braided cord is not easily broken."** *Husband, wife and the Holy Spirit in the center is a recipe for a fruitful marriage with a promise of longevity.*

On our wedding day, my Pastor wanted our marriage to be unshakeable so much that the foundation of the earth could not move it.

So on December 6, 1986, an exuberant young bride and her husband tied the knot at Double Portion Church in Northport, Alabama USA. Though there were few in attendance, the heavenly host was certainly present! The sun shone brightly but rain soon began to fall causing an interruption in our nuptials.

My young brother Archie had recently obtained his driver's license and had virtually no experience driving in the city of Northport and Tuscaloosa. The inevitable happened, an accident that prevented a portion of my family from attending the wedding!

I sat in the reception hall with a tear streaked face wondering exactly how to proceed. My Pastor had the answer, "The show must go on Sis Rhonda." And so it did. We wed in our small chapel in an intimate setting with International guests intermingling along the aisles and also just inside the vestibule amidst our Southern interracial folk. My husband's best man was from Paris, another guest from Mexico, the flower girl and ring bearer's Mom was from Puerto Rico, and the list goes on.

At the close of our reception, Clement and I thrilled that we were finally married, walked towards our sports car oblivious to the fact that God had smiled down on us. A supernatural occurrence took place. A rainbow appeared mysteriously on a photo taken by my sister Sarah. She had preceded me in becoming born again and was on fire and full of the Spirit.

Rainbow from Heaven

Photo untouched

As the small crowd of "amateur paparazzi" snapped our departure, none of us knew the magnitude of the angelic host that might have been present during that single event. It is worth mentioning that we possess no professional photos as our photographer never contacted us after the wedding!

God collaborated with Pastor Moss in His prophetic Words----"Lord, bind this couple up tight, don't let anyone or anything separate them!"

It was a couple years later before Sarah would give me the photo and many years more before the Lord revealed to me our wedding covenant.

I don't believe either Sarah or I truly understood the signification of the photograph until the Spirit so generously revealed it to me.

The Lord first showed me the appearance of the rainbow after the flood in Genesis 9:1, **"I have set my rainbow in the clouds, and it will be the sign of the covenant between me and the earth."** *He promised he would never destroy mankind again by water. Whenever the rainbow appeared in the sky, it would serve as a token of a covenant between God and the human race! What a promise from a mighty God!*

I had left my family in the United States to follow my husband to the continent of Africa. This promise was relevant at all times as danger lurked on every side, yet God's covenant stood.

God revealed further our wedding covenant to me in Isaiah 54:10, ***"Though the mountains be shaken and the hills be removed, yet my unfailing love for you will not be shaken nor my covenant of peace be removed says the Lord, who has compassion on you."***

Through our union, God would reach back to His promise in Genesis 9:13 and Isaiah 54:10 and extend these blessings to our posterity. Our eldest, Alesea would marry and produce her first son whom we named Olivier. His name was taken from the story of Noah who released the dove after the flood to bring back life the second time in the form of an olive branch (see Genesis 8:11). Olivier's name stems from the word olive and signifies life.

My hope is that as you read these faith filled pages, you will become one with God's Word and receive life! 'Release the Dove' has been written from a perspective of a desperate grandmother who would do all she could to preserve the life of her grand-son. It would take courage; it would take defying the reality of what is seen and heard; it would take a stead-fast resolve and me reaching down to all I have learned over the years through my faith walk with the Lord.

It has been a journey with the protection of the rainbow covering my family with a covenant of peace. In all we experienced through this ordeal, we remained in peace (Read Isaiah 26.3).

'Release the Dove' is a story of hope and abundant life. My prayer is that as each of my readers explore this book; he or she will find faith to endure whatever trial you are going through. I release the Dove of Peace over each and every one of you in Jesus Mighty Name!

In His Service,

Rhonda Wilson-Dikoko

Table of Contents

Foreword………………………………………………………………	2
Dedication……………………………………………………………..	3
Tribute to Olivier: Infinity Love……………………………………...	4
Prelude………………………………………………………………..	5
Table of Contents…………………………………………………….	9
Acknowledgements…………………………………………………..	10
Introduction……………………………………………………………	11
1. Choosing a Name………………………………………..	12
2. Acclimation to KL………………………………………..	16
3. The weekend prior to Olivier's Sickness…………………	18
4. The fever………………………………………………..	19
5. A diagnosis……………………………………………..	24
6. Capable doctors…………………………………………	40
7. A risk of faith…………………………………………..	42
8. A word on faith…………………………………………	46
9. Easter eve……………………………………………….	49
10. The big turnaround……………………………………..	52
11. Talitha Koum-Arise…………………………………….	58
12. Olivier's Resurrection………………………………….	61
13. The failed test………………………………………….	68
14. Recovery………………………………………………..	75
15. Paradigm shift………………………………………….	79
16. Alesea and Sanaa's arrival in Singapore………………..	81
17. Return to KL…………………………………………...	83
18. Completing fourth grade………………………………	85
19. Olivier's birthday party……………………………….	86
Postlude……………………………………………………………...	89
Praise Report………………………………………………………..	95
Final Reflections by Shola………………………………………….	96
Appendix……………………………………………………………..	99
References…………………………………………………………..	103
About the author……………………………………………………	104

Acknowledgements

I would like to show my sincere gratitude to Elmine Knight who willingly and lovingly offered her time to edit these pages to bring forth a work of art that would bless us all. I am indebted to her for time spent beautifying my pictures and giving such a professional look to this book. Elmine was the one who said, 'write, I will edit'. She was a loyal companion throughout this endeavor. Thank you so much Elmine!

I am so thankful to Barb Angell for her "fresh pair" of eyes that helped to make my message more fluid. I really appreciate you and your precious family!

I am so grateful to Pastor Lisa E. Great, a seasoned writer and author; my mentee and encourager who also served as an advisor as I wrote this book.

Nicole Voelkel, though you came in at the tail end; your wisdom and suggestions about this publication were very valuable to me. Thank you so much!

Sincere thanks to Danielle Dikoko who helped design the cover and beautify the pages of this book.

I wish to thank Shereen & William Costley and their family who selflessly loved us through this ordeal hosting us whilst we were in Singapore.

Much gratitude goes to Clement, my loving husband who believed in me and trusted that I would hear from God.

I will be forever grateful to Alesea N. Dikoko-Woodgett and Carmelo (Mel) Woodgett who so graciously agreed that I tell this story and who have trusted us to co-parent Olivier for many years now.

I would like to applaud Olivier – You are a brave soul. You have taught us so much during your short years on this earth bringing us such joy at every turn. Being so full of life and not afraid to follow your grand-parents to the ends of the earth. May the Lord God Almighty complete the great work He has started in you. May you fulfill your destiny.

Simply,

Koko

Introduction

Olivier came to us at a time we least expected. Our eldest daughter Alesea was entering her junior year of University therefore my husband, Clement and I were devastated. It was as if all the dreams we had for our eldest vanished into thin air. Out of anger and pride, I vowed not to take part in our grandchild's upbringing but to make sure Alesea and her boyfriend Carmelo took care of their own child!

My best friend Cathy Michonet, scoffed at my remark, laughingly saying, *"Rhonda, I don't know who you're fooling girl, you're going to have that child in your arms as soon as he's born!"*

I could not fathom that my own child would have a baby out of wedlock! Our family's belief system is deeply rooted in the love of Christ. Our children have been raised in this Faith. The Lord did a marvelous work in my life in this regard; urging me to be loving, kind and *not* judgmental. To just embrace my oldest and let her know I was there for her.

As disappointed as we were, my husband made a radical decision that we would not force the young couple to marry. But as the Lord would have it, they wed on their own accord when Olivier was one year old. It was their choice, their decision and that was paramount.

Shortly after her engagement, Alesea reminded me of a prophecy she had been given concerning her future husband. He would be from an island and it so happens that our son in law's mother was from the Philippines! To make matters even more interesting Carmelo and Alesea resembled each other when they first met--so much so that they could be mistaken for brother and sister! When Olivier was a baby, we couldn't decide who he resembled the most because of the similarities in looks and personalities!

Carmelo turned out to be the dream son in law every mother would want for her daughter; intelligent, caring, a good husband and father as well as a good provider. Our disappointment quickly dissipated as we got to know this young man and welcomed him wholeheartedly into our family.

Chapter 1

<u>Choosing a Name</u>

My daughter gave me the distinct privilege of helping her choose a name for their son. My husband is originally from Brazzaville, Congo. In his culture, names are meaningful. You gave a person a name according to who you wanted him or her to become in life. Never the less, while I lived in Congo, I found people with less desirable names such as Modest. The Pastor there changed his name to Prosper. Or like my neighbor's son whose name in his native tongue meant; *'destined to fail'*. Though he was a bright young man and had taught himself how to speak English, he was not successful in life. Who on earth would give their child a name which might influence his future to such a devastating extent?

I sought the face of the Lord to come up with a fitting name for our first grandson-- a distinguishing name which would well define his future. Alesea and I both liked the sound of *'Olivier'*. I loved the way my friend Cathy rolled this name off her tongue. The name Olivier is from French origin and means *'from the olive tree'*.

Being Christian, I specifically thought of the dove in Genesis 8:11 which Noah sent out to determine whether there was life on earth. The second time the dove returned with a freshly plucked olive leaf in his beak signifying life was present upon the earth which had been previously flooded. So Olivier's name is synonymous with life.

Olivier arrived on August 3, 2005. The date is most vivid in my mind as I had returned to the States for his delivery in Jacksonville, Alabama. This was the year that Mega-Fest ('Woman Thou Art Loosed Conference', by T.D. Jakes) would take place in Atlanta, Georgia, I planned on attending with my friends who traveled from Gabon, Africa, for this great event. I prayed that Alesea would have a safe delivery in time for me to attend the conference and God granted us our heart's desire!

From the moment Olivier was born, he brought joy to my soul and to that of my family's. My husband, Clement, arrived in the USA shortly after his birth and from the moment he laid eyes on him, Olivier stole his heart! The proud parents quickly acclimatized to having a child around but treated him like 'one of them'. When he was much older, they spoke to him like a 'college student' therefore the first thing you'll notice when meeting Olivier for the first time is how well versed he is; able to converse on multiple levels. He possesses knowledge about certain things far beyond his mortal years.

Shortly after Olivier's parents married and his first birthday, we took him to live with us in Nigeria to allow Alesea and Carmelo to complete their last year at JSU (Jacksonville State University) in relative peace and tranquility.

In Nigeria, Olivier was doted on by a nanny I secured for him and the house help. It was there that he was taught to take naps on his own and become a little independent 'thinker'.

Unfortunately, his time in Nigeria was short lived as we were evacuated to Bordeaux, France. Our twins, Danielle and Clement Jr., were 11years old at the time and attending The International School of Bordeaux while living with host parents. Our son, Clement Jr. had experienced difficulty acclimatizing to life in France and therefore had returned to live with us in Port Harcourt, Nigeria, prior to the evacuation.

So it was a natural decision for me to choose to live in Bordeaux where Clement Jr. would continue his bilingual studies with his sister. Together we bonded with Olivier throughout the cold winter months. Danielle remained with the host family while Clement Sr. continued to work in Nigeria. I had the full responsibility of taking care of our grandson, Olivier.

The winter months soon ended to reveal a spring full of life and vitality. We decided to return to the USA and place the twins in school there. We moved to Atlanta, Georgia and Olivier returned to live with his parents.

As expatriates our lives are always on the go, bringing uncertainty at every turn. Our stay in Atlanta, Georgia, was also temporary. Clement was relocated to The Hague where we spent 18 months. Olivier and his mom visited us there over the Christmas holidays of 2008.

During the summer of 2009, the company my husband works for, relocated us to Malaysia. Alesea had returned to graduate school and we decided that Olivier should join us in Malaysia. We found a lovely nanny, Rose, from the Philippines to take care of him. Rose spoiled him rotten and catered to his every whim.

Olivier was four years old and attended Children's House Kindergarten. He was dropped off every day by Grandpa and the driver. Every weekend, he and Grandpa were at one theme park or another. Their plan was to visit every fun park in Malaysia together!

The twins debuted 9th grade at ISKL. Danielle had begged us to have a pet so I finally succumbed to getting her a beautiful well-mannered Golden Retriever named Bailey whom we inherited from a friend. This four month old puppy and Olivier became fast friends romping in the back yard and spending every waking moment together.

Olivier had been taking steroids for asthma, but up till this point had not had any episodes. However with Bailey's fur and dander, we started experiencing more and more asthmatic attacks.

By now, back in the USA, Alesea was pregnant with their second child Sanaa and took a break from graduate school. Olivier returned to live with his parents.

Olivier's three year old sister, Sanaa, was instrumental in his speedy recovery. She kept him motivated and said to him matter-of-factly with full blown hand movements "You're going to be okay, Olivier, you're going to be okay."

Ours is an extended family concept therefore, it is not unusual for us to assist in raising our grandchildren, nieces or nephews. In fact, a good friend remarked what a blessing it is for Clement and I to still be so young yet have the opportunity to partake in our grandchildren's upbringing. I started seeing it as the blessing that it was!

Psalm 128; The Living Bible (TLB), says:
"Blessings on all who reverence and trust the Lord—on all who obey him! [2] **Their reward shall be prosperity and happiness.** [3] **Your wife shall be contented in your home. And look at all those children! There they sit around the dinner table as vigorous and healthy as young olive trees.** [4] **That is God's reward to those who reverence and trust him.** [5] **May the Lord continually bless you with heaven's blessings as**

well as with human joys. ⁶May you live to enjoy your grandchildren! And may God bless Israel!"

In summer 2014, Alesea and her family made a major decision to return to Huntsville, Alabama, where she had previously begun her graduate degree. She had determined to complete her degree and enter into the workforce. With the support of her husband, they made the transition.

Sanaa, their toddler was manageable but finding an appropriate school for Olivier would prove to be complicated. They searched frantically for the best private school for Olivier that would also be affordable for their budget.

On one of our outings together, Olivier revealed to me his desire to return to Kuala Lumpur, Malaysia. I was so surprised and taken aback. After careful discussion with his parents and Grandpa, we decided to bring him back with us. This would afford Alesea the necessary time needed for her to complete her degree. It was planned that upon completion of graduate school, Olivier would settle back in with his parents. He would only have one year with us as we suspected we would also be leaving Malaysia after six and a half years.

The move to Huntsville turned out to be a blessing in disguise for Olivier's parents. Carmelo decided to return to work with a sub-contractor for NASA (National Aeronautics and Space Administration).

Chapter 2

<u>Acclimation to KL</u>

Olivier had a smooth landing into ISKL. He turned 9 in August of 2014 and not only had a party with his family and friends before leaving the USA but also had a mini celebration with "KoKo" and Grandpa to welcome him to life the second time around in Asia!

Koko is Olivier's favorite nickname for me. It's actually taken from my husband's dialect and is the name used for grandmother. Being such a young grandmother, the nickname appealed to me! We started using it from the moment he was born!

Olivier soon acclimatized to school, made friends quickly and participated in sports such as judo and soccer. He enjoyed play dates and weekend outings with his friends and Grandpa.

Life was almost the same as his earlier stay with us except the twins were off to university but his nanny, Rose, was still there!

In retrospect, I've often thought about the circumstances around Olivier's return to us. We received blessings from his parents and he obtained favor in receiving a place at ISKL. However, when we were returning to KL from the USA over Christmas of 2014, Olivier and I were detained for a long while at the airline counter in Atlanta, Georgia. There were several issues with his passport that almost left us grounded in Atlanta. After serious negotiations with the management of the airline, we were allowed to travel.

In hind sight, was this a warning that he should have been left behind? Was this a way of the Lord protecting him from the inevitable? The airline's reasoning was unfounded. After years of traveling, I knew the law and was able to get on the flight but we literally had to run for it!

Chapter 3

<u>The weekend Prior to Olivier's Sickness</u>

One weekend on March 14, 2015 there was a hot air balloon show in Putrajaya. Clement decided to take Olivier and friends of ours. Oliver's classmates were also planning on being there. They met up at Putrajaya and had a fun filled afternoon.

How little did I know that this weekend would include the fateful day, the start of Olivier's illness and the test of my faith?

This would be the very first time that Olivier would be in close proximity with hundreds of Malaysians. He did not have sufficient immunity against diseases or bacteria that lurked in the waters of Malaysia.

Chapter 4

<u>The Fever</u>

On Saturday, the 21st of March 2015 Olivier came to me holding up a thermometer. "Look Koko," he said, "I'm sick, I've got a temperature."

The thermometer registered 102 °F (38.8°C). That was the very first time he had ever had such a high fever since coming to live with us in September 2014.

The week prior, Olivier had been well although the week preceding that, as a precautionary measure, I had put him on his nebulizer after he attended a hot air balloon event in Putrajaya. He had gone with his grandpa and had met up with his classmates; arriving home his clothes had been a little damp after their balloon adventure.

In my family, I practice prevention and often prefer homeopathic solutions to pharmaceuticals. The Bible says in Revelations 22:2, ***"the leaves are used for the healing of the nation."*** I truly believe that!

Being a minister of the gospel, I also strongly believe in divine healing. But when it's your grandchild you tend to do things a little differently. So on that fateful Saturday morning, I gave Olivier an oral fever reducer and started pushing fluids which he was reluctant to drink. I went to an early Morning Prayer service at a Chinese church and returned home to find that Olivier's fever persisted. I gave him another oral medication, pushed fluids and left him resting in his room busy playing his favorite electronic games.

Being quite fatigued myself; I took a nap and woke up to find that Olivier had gone out with his grandpa as they usually do on the weekend. My motherly instinct was on high alert. I was a little annoyed that Clement had taken the child out without my knowing whether or not his fever had subsided. We had a dinner party planned that night at a restaurant with friends therefore I had initially thought I'd leave Olivier with our neighbors. It had also rained that day and I was concerned whether Olivier had kept dry.

I spoke to Clement by phone and he reassured me Olivier was fine and would attend the dinner with us. He was already at the restaurant so our guests and I joined them there. Upon arriving at Susie's Corner, the most famous open air steak restaurant in Kuala Lumpur, and seeing Olivier, I knew immediately that his fever was back. He sat lethargic on a plastic chair with his head on the table. His eyes were dull and his skin was clammy to touch. The smoke from the barbecue and the damp air further irritated his symptoms. Throughout the evening he grew more and more lethargic, barely touching his food and nagged me to go home.

"When are we going Koko?" he said, visibly exhausted with blood shot eyes from the smoke of the barbecue.

"Soon my *cucu*, soon", I said, using the Malay word for grandchild.

We left as soon as the meal was over. Once home, I gave him another dose of medication to reduce his fever and tucked him into bed.

Sunday morning, March 22nd, Olivier wasn't any better so I decided to take him to Prince Court Hospital (PCH). Clement felt we should attend church and take him to hospital afterwards. Despite fever, Olivier still had an appetite and loved playing his video games. However, he refused to take in fluids.

I understood at this point that this was no ordinary malady and started praying seriously for my grandson.

Immediately following church service, we had lunch in one of the restaurants on the ground floor of the building. True to his nature, Olivier ate his meal with gusto. He had always been a good eater, therefore I still felt encouraged since his appetite was intact. I offered him an assortment of drinks, but he was hard-pressed to sip any. We hurried to PCH from there.

At PCH, he was received relatively quickly in the emergency room. Olivier shivered beneath a thin blanket while a battery of tests was done. The results yielded negative results including dengue which I seriously suspected. Dengue is a mosquito borne virus which had ravaged 100 deaths to date in Kuala Lumpur[1].

After a couple of hours, Olivier was sent home with a bag full of medication including oral antibiotics. Despite his cocktail of medication, Olivier's fever raged throughout the night.

Shortly after coming to live with us, Olivier had been baptized. So at 3 a.m., I decided to serve him communion and we prayed. His fever broke around 7 a.m. Rose sponged him off and changed his pajamas which had been drenched in sweat and finally he succumbed to sleep. Needless to say, I kept him home from school that Monday.

I am a substitute nurse at ISKL where Olivier attended. I knew there had not been an influx of viruses in his grade.

I messaged a friend of mine from the Middle East who had worked in a government hospital on various wards for many years. She was also a mid-wife but was very knowledgeable about children's illnesses.

I told her about Olivier's re-occurring fevers that spiked throughout the day. She recommended a suppository as well as a concoction of leaves to boil. I didn't relish the thought of fighting my way through Kuala Lumpur's 6 p.m. traffic to go to an open market in order to purchase the herbs required for the concoction. However, I knew the back way to a pharmacy near our high school campus and so rushed there to get the suppository.

Ironically, I met my supervisor, the head nurse of ISKL, and spoke to her about Olivier's condition. She empathized with me and agreed with my course of action.

My midwife friend had recommended a paracetamol suppository but after explaining to the pharmacist my grandson's condition, she suggested Diclofenac₁ saying she generally gave it to her baby and it reduced the fever immediately.

Not being familiar with its generic name, I read the inside pamphlet and told her that the information did not specify the product actually was a fever reducer but she assured me it was. This raised a red flag in my mind. This was a certified pharmacist who used the medication on her baby therefore I thought for sure it would be safe enough for my big boy.

I dashed back home avoiding much of the traffic on the main street. Sure enough, after coaxing Olivier into letting me administer the suppository his fever broke right away! I was relieved and we all got a good night's sleep.

Yet the next morning which was Tuesday March 24, Olivier appeared a little giddy and complained of leg pain. Although his fever had subsided after taking the medication the night before he said he had felt disoriented and confused during the night.

After showering he required assistance getting up from the floor where he had sat to pull on his clothes. Both Rose and I were alarmed and baffled by his disposition and went for a second time to PCH.

I was at a loss at what to do to get him to drink. In the morning, I had run to the supermarket to purchase coconut water which is an invigorating rehydrating drink. I also bought popsicles and plenty of juices but to my chagrin, my little man wasn't having any of it. Out of desperation, I threatened Intravenous (IV) Fluids which he told me he preferred than to have to drink all those fluids!

I requested prayers from my intercessors and friends. The doctors conducted a more complete battery of tests and only found that Olivier was dehydrated as I suspected. I reported that his fever had been persistent since Saturday. I also relayed the previous nights' experience. This time they sent me home with Voltaren suppositories and asked me to continue with the Augmentin antibiotic.

Again, Olivier's fever subsided however he seemed more and more lethargic. His appetite was still good but I couldn't get him to eat a soft diet either! He started to vomit. His fluid intake was also not sufficient enough to stave off a fever. He preferred solid foods but was becoming more and more nauseated from the intake of so many different medications. I felt that a soft diet would be better for him.

Olivier has weekly calls with his parents, but I tried to prevent undue worry as I knew how stressful university could be for Alesea and starting a new job at NASA was for Carmelo. Nevertheless, I called to enlist their help in getting Olivier to drink more fluids as well as to encourage him to get well soon. He nodded to his parents plea (while on the phone) for him to drink a sufficient amount of fluids. However; he was uncharacteristically quiet.

Wednesday morning, March 25th, we needed to go to the Embassy of the United States to renew Olivier's passport. We planned a trip to Sri Lanka for Spring break and I was still hopeful we could go. Olivier mustered enough energy for our short drive to the embassy. Clement drove us there parking in the lot close to the embassy's entrance. Olivier was very weak, walking slowly with our assistance. Upon arrival, we were told the consulate section was closed for the day! Clement went back to the parking lot to fetch the car while I sat giving Olivier sips of juice I had brought with me as well as food for him anticipating a long wait at the embassy.

Having worked at U.S. embassies twice in my life, I knew that there was always a skeleton crew on standby who were able to assist Americans. So I approached security once more and miraculously, they allowed us in! I informed Clement by phone and ascended the steps to the consulate section with a very fatigued Olivier in tow. He didn't have fever but was visibly affected by the toll the medicine, sickness and disease were having on his body. By the grace of God, we somehow managed to get through the passport process and Olivier endured the interview although he had to lie down on the chairs while waiting.

In hindsight, we were forever grateful that the passport process was successful as this would be the last time Olivier would be cognitively well and physically strong enough to endure this process. Unknown to us at the time, God's favor had been with us from that moment forward. Little did we know that we would need his renewed passport for Singapore!

Chapter 5

<u>**A Diagnosis**</u>

The next day was Thursday, March 26th. Olivier's fevers were ongoing. He only experienced a short respite after his suppository. This time, I decided to take him to his old pediatrician at Gleneagles Hospital, another hospital in Kuala Lumpur (KL), Malaysia. When Olivier lived with us a few years back, a local pediatrician had been instrumental in weaning Olivier from his medication for asthma. Upon arrival in the pediatrician's office, he remembered Olivier right away. He decided more tests were necessary to ascertain the true nature of Olivier's illness. I actually insisted on hospitalization due to dehydration. The wards were full but his staff managed to find a spot on the Women and Children's ward. I felt a sigh of relief that Olivier was in the hands of this particular pediatrician, a very much trusted physician.

Friday, March 27th, Olivier was started on a drip and the next day his pediatrician triumphantly revealed the culprit causing the raging fevers; it was Mycoplasma pneumonia, a human pathogen. It was a bacterial infection and not viral as had been earlier suspected.

Mycoplasma pneumonia (MP) sometimes referred to as 'walking pneumonia' is a contagious respiratory infection. The disease spreads easily through contact with respiratory fluids, and it causes regular epidemics. The most common sign of infection is a dry cough. Untreated or severe cases can have symptoms affecting the heart and nervous system. In rare cases, MP can be fatal. Diagnosis is difficult in the early stages of MP because there are few unusual symptoms. As the disease progresses, imaging and laboratory tests may be able to detect it. Doctors use antibiotics to treat MP. If antibiotics aren't effective at treating MP, you may need intravenous medications[2].

I was glad that I had brought Olivier to this doctor. I had confidence in him and respected his judgement. Appropriate treatment was commenced immediately but I didn't see the huge improvement that he predicted.

Oliver was still experiencing high fevers and using two types of fever reducers! He was becoming less and less responsive. He was definitely not himself. His constant companion, which was his iPhone, was no longer of any interest to him. He retreated into his shell and allowed the illness to ravage his body. After one week of fevers, it seems there was no fight left in him.

As I sleep very poorly in a chair, Rose, Olivier's nanny stayed with him in the evenings and Clement and I took shifts during the day. He also had an entourage of nurses who were very helpful and attentive to his care.

Saturday, March 28, marked one week since the commencement of the malady. Although the day was uneventful in itself, Olivier started experiencing different symptoms such as headaches and nausea. Clement and I camped at his bedside during the day while Rose returned home to rest.

His doctor came every day to see his patients and reported that he planned on releasing Olivier on Sunday. Given Olivier's present state, I was doubtful.

On Sunday, March 29, Olivier began to have serious issues with blurred and double vision. The previous evening, his nanny reported that he started hallucinating, talking to himself and imagining his deceased grandmother at his bedside.

Naturally, this new condition was very alarming for the nanny as well as for us. We asked the doctors to perform a cat scan on Olivier's brain, which they did. The results were not remarkable and in fact were completely normal.

By Monday, March 30, Olivier had a peculiar gait; he became more and more paranoid when asked to stand or to go to the toilet. His eyes were completely uncontrollable and rolled back in his head frequently. His doctor sent Olivier to the ophthalmologist to determine whether his eyesight was normal.

In the afternoon, a nurse's aide took Olivier to see the ophthalmologist via wheelchair. I walked alongside him talking quietly, not able to tolerate the pitiful glances and stares directed at my grandson. Olivier was oblivious to this attention.

Poor Olivier had become very animated at this point. In an attempt to keep him in touch with reality, we were planning a visit with his best friend. I had made the call since Olivier's vision did not allow him to focus long enough to dial the numbers. He and his buddy spoke briefly while scheming their next play date. This was the only shred of normalcy in Olivier's world. Everything else seemed surreal as I waited to be awakened any moment from this nightmare. Olivier's best friend's Mom wasn't able to bring him for a visit. I secretly felt better with her decision as I didn't relish anyone seeing Olivier in this awkward condition.

Olivier's vision steadied long enough to allow him to read signs posted on the wall of the doctor's office but he commented to me that he had double vision.

Although we were ushered in to see the eye doctor relatively quickly, it seemed like an eternity to me. While waiting, I tried to avert the pitiful glances of the other patients present in the waiting area. I placed Olivier's wheelchair in a manner whereby he was facing the wall and his back was to the other patients.

My thoughts ran rampant. Why were we there anyway? Why was Olivier so ill? What was happening to my grandson? All of these questions were running through my mind at break neck speed. I wondered why his doctor had recommended he see the specialist instead of the specialist coming to see Olivier on his ward. I was becoming increasingly agitated at the side long glances and whispered concerns I was experiencing around us.

Suddenly Olivier's name was called. The door to the ophthalmologist opened wide enough to allow the wheelchair to enter. Needless to say, the doctor was unable to perform the entire exam; however, he concluded Olivier's eyesight was normal and his blurred and double vision was only a manifestation of the illness. He said once Mycoplasma cleared up, Olivier's eyesight would be back to normal. The doctor reported he'd never seen this type of reaction with MP.

We returned to the ward dejected and feeling hopeless. I felt as if we had hit yet another brick wall. Symptoms were very uncharacteristic of MP. Had he been misdiagnosed?

His doctor now suspected Opsoclonus Myoclonus Syndrome (OMS), also known as Opsoclonus-Myoclonus-Ataxia (OMA), a rare neurological disorder of unknown causes which appears to be the result of an autoimmune process involving the nervous system. It is an extremely rare condition, affecting as few as one in 10,000,000 people per year. It affects two to three percent of children with neuroblastoma and has been reported to occur with celiac disease[3].

Opsoclonus refers to the eyes. In Olivier's case, it presented as an alternate involuntary muscular contraction and relaxation in rapid succession. His eye balls turned uncontrollably.

Myoclonus is a spasmodic jerky contraction of groups of muscles and in Olivier's case referred to his legs. This was the cause of his unsteady gait.

For example, hiccups are a form of myoclonus. So are the sudden jerks, or 'sleep starts,' you may experience just before falling asleep. These forms of Myoclonus occur in healthy people and rarely present a problem.

Most often, Myoclonus occurs as a result of a nervous system (neurological) disorder, such as epilepsy, or of a metabolic condition, or as a reaction to a medication.

Despite my determination to keep people away, a number of my friends including Malay friends of ours and ladies from my Oasis Bible Study group, stopped by the hospital to pray, sing hymns and bring comfort to us. A friend brought a teddy bear which was to remain with Olivier throughout his hospitalization.

Others wanted to come but visits were discouraged due to Olivier's symptoms and increasingly abnormal behavior. I particularly did not want him seen in this pitiful state.

My Malay friends were quite alarmed at the site of Olivier's condition asking multiple questions which I didn't have the answer to. This was precisely the reason I had dissuaded visits. I didn't want Olivier pitied and I also did not want to lose hope.

Following this latest development, Olivier's doctor ordered a magnetic resonance imaging (MRI) to be carried out immediately that evening. It was performed on him under a mild sedative. This allowed Olivier a brief respite and a couple of hours of rest afterwards. Again the results were deemed normal, yet in actuality Olivier's condition had worsened.

Our senior pastor from The Ambassador's International Church, Reverend Amos, stopped by to visit and to pray for Olivier. He came to find us in the X-ray section of the hospital right after the MRI. Although Olivier was unable to respond being too drowsy after the sedative, it was a comfort to have the pastor come by. He followed us up to the room and spent some moments of prayer before bidding us farewell and giving encouraging words to us. We were extremely grateful for all these heroic acts of faith.

The next day, Tuesday, March 31st, I had a standing appointment with a walking buddy on Tuesdays, but had to cancel as I needed to see the doctor regarding the way forward. When I phoned my friend to let her know I wasn't available to walk, she was surprised Olivier wasn't any better and suggested I seek treatment in Singapore. I thanked her for her concern tucking her suggestion away in the back of my mind as I rushed to the hospital to meet the doctor.

Arriving there I found Olivier's behavior had become increasingly bizarre. He was talking to himself and imagining people were around. He became very talkative and had insomnia along with rambling inappropriate speech. Olivier was still lucid and knew who we all were but his eyes were now uncontrollable and he was having great difficulty walking. Needless to say, this was like a bad nightmare for us all. We had gone from possibly being discharged on Sunday to considering evacuating to Singapore on Tuesday!

The doctor's next choice of action was to begin Olivier on an immunoglobulin treatment as it was becoming increasingly clear that Olivier most likely had experienced an autoimmune reaction to his treatment. I was very confident in Olivier's pediatrician who was extremely dedicated to his patients sometimes working seven days a week and visiting Olivier three or four times a day when necessary.

Indeed, the doctor and his staff were very caring; we had no doubt they were committed to Olivier's wellbeing. But his doctor was at a loss how to proceed without aid of a neurologist. He needed a neurologist to follow up on Olivier's treatment, but none would take his case. Out of 35 years of working as a pediatrician including working years in intensive care unit (ICU), he admitted NEVER having seen a case like my grandson's, even with treating as many as three or four Mycoplasma cases per week! In fact, he exclaimed, many of the cases did not require hospitalization and sometimes no treatment is followed!

Olivier born in the United Sates, had not acquired immunity to tropical illnesses and was unable to fight this quite 'common bug' coupled with the fact that he had been on steroid medication for asthma for several years which had suppressed his immune system.

Olivier's doctor was considering transferring him to a teaching hospital in Kuala Lumpur. While I trusted this doctor completely, I did not relish the idea of Olivier going to a local hospital and being treated as a specimen by the many interns who would no doubt be practicing there. I was concerned that his immune system would be further compromised. I felt at a loss about what to do. Then I thought of my friend's suggestion to evacuate to Singapore. I now felt that this advice was Holy Spirit inspired.

After careful discussion with my husband, I requested Olivier's doctor to transfer him to Singapore.

Wheels were put in motion both spiritually and medically to make this transfer happen ASAP. I asked my walking buddy Carol to rally the Oasis Bible Study Group to pray for Olivier's case. I rushed home to grab a few items including our passports.

Clement informed Oliver's parents of the devastating news. Both Alesea and Carmelo were afraid for their little boy, but I assured them nothing would happen to Olivier while with me. I must have received that assurance from God to speak those words so boldly and fearlessly.

Alesea and Carmelo though worried, garnered enough strength to get prayer chains going in the United States while Carol got the Oasis Bible Study Group praying in Kuala Lumpur. Our friends and Clément's extended family were also praying in The Congo, Gabon, France, Belgium and other countries too numerous to recall.

The doctor worked for several hours organizing a transfer for Olivier via ambulance. He was concerned that a flight would be much too dangerous for him. I liaised with the insurance company to have accurate coverage in place.

Finally around 14:30 it was time to go. Olivier's doctor came to bid us farewell giving me a sign of hope. Hugging Olivier he said, "We'll see you back here in two weeks Olivier, okay." He patted Olivier on his cheeks, bade me Godspeed and left. Again, I was touched by his outward show of affection towards his patient.

Another doctor had been assigned to accompany us. He came to Olivier's room to introduce himself. The nurses also came to prepare Olivier's exit via ambulance. Many of the nurses on the ward came to see us off in tears. I was overwhelmed by their show of emotion for Olivier during his departure.

Olivier was expertly transferred from the hospital bed to the gurney. As we navigated our way through the hospital past the emergency room sympathetic eyes bore down upon us everywhere. Clement and Rose were in shambles, I kept my composure as to not alarm Olivier of the degree of his illness. It was as if we were already in mourning.

Olivier was seemingly unaware of what was happening although I kept him alert and up to speed on his whereabouts. I patiently explained that we were leaving Gleneagles Hospital to seek further care for him in Singapore. We would be traveling by ambulance. He loved cars and could name just about any car on the road, but now he was not up to playing that game.

Olivier had been to Singapore a few times prior and equated Singapore to 'fun times' at the Night Safari or Sentosa Island. I longed for it to be a fun trip instead of an evacuation. I let him know that we would be going to the hospital there. He nodded his head, his eyes, now vacant stirring at some unseen object in the air, his pupils were still doing 'their own thing' dancing and rotating as if in orbit.

The transfer was swift into the ambulance. The driver, the ambulance assistant and the doctor first settled Olivier before I bade a quick farewell to Clement and Rose hopping in the ambulance without a backward glance. I willed myself not to breakdown as I knew I needed to be strong for the long road ahead.

My emotions had taken back seat while my spirit was the commander of my soul and was being led by the promptings of the Holy Spirit.

I busied myself with the seat belt flap as the ambulance jerked into breakneck speed sirens hissing as traffic cleared the way on Jalan Ampang, gliding towards the highway leading out of Kuala Lumpur towards Singapore.

The ambulance ride seemed surreal. Hearing the sirens, I wondered about the urgency of the emergency. I was jolted back to reality understanding we were the cause. I felt as if I was having an 'out of body experience'. This catastrophe was happening to someone else and not me.

The further we distanced ourselves from Kuala Lumpur, the lighter in spirit I became. Joy flooded my soul and hope leapt up in my spirit performing somersaults in the chambers of my heart.

There was nary a visible reason for the change in my heart except that faith was springing forth. In the natural, Oliver's condition was the same if not worst. He talked excessively of strange things, his eyes rolled back in his head. He was unable to remain still, but kept trying to leave the stretcher he was strapped to.

Yet an expanse of darkness seemed to separate us from Kuala Lumpur as we gained speed towards Singapore.

The six hours to Singapore were not tedious for me. It seemed as if we were translated from one place to another at the speed of light! I was no longer thinking of myself or my comforts, but was in survival mode. My emotions had taken back seat while my spirit was the commander of my soul and was being led by the promptings of the Holy Spirit.

We only made a brief stop during which time Olivier indicated that he needed to urinate. The accompanying doctor assured me we would be in Singapore in no time and would be able to attend to Olivier's needs properly upon arrival. He was strapped to the stretcher for the duration of the trip.

> *It was as if God had draped a cloak of peace about my shoulders and I was experiencing Kingdom favor.*

We had been through Singapore's immigration on several occasions and knew that the process could be thorough. This time things went relatively smooth. There were no comments about Olivier's passport expiring in three months. We were allowed to continue our journey in relative quiet. (I had hoped Olivier would get his new passport in less than two weeks in time to leave Singapore back to KL).

The ambulance driver had difficulty locating the hospital thus I became increasingly concerned about Olivier being uncomfortable for such a long time. Finally the global positioning system (GPS) yielded results and we pulled up to the emergency room of the Blue Eagle's Hospital (BEH) (Not the real name). This hospital was the largest, specializing in healthcare for women and Children in Singapore [4].

The staff of BEH worked quickly alongside the Gleneagles team to efficiently get Olivier out of the ambulance and onto their emergency room bed. We were overwhelmed by medical staff and the dreaded interns who all assisted simultaneously to change Olivier into their BEH hospital gown, and take his vital signs all the while they were asking an array of questions which Olivier answered with a rapidity and accuracy that proved he was still coherent. The exchange was done swiftly.

I said my goodbyes to the kind Gleneagles doctor and staff who had accompanied me and now I was left all alone. Yet, I didn't feel alone. I felt a presence of tranquility about me. It was as if God had draped a cloak of peace about my shoulders and I was experiencing Kingdom favor.

interns, nurses gathered about his bed checking his vitals and devouring his doctor's notes from Gleneagles Hospital. Yet they were relentless in their interviewing. The same questions were asked several times to Olivier to ascertain his alertness. His answers were constant. He knew where he was, he knew who he was, his age, where he attended school as well as the names of his friends. His speech sometimes inappropriate was now fast and jittery, his eyes darting from one doctor to the other ordering them to leave him alone. Perhaps he was tired and scared, using this as a protective mechanism against his fright. I reassured him the best I could.

At last we found ourselves on the High Dependency Ward where the nurses were friendly and helpful. The doctors ordered a lumbar puncture/spinal tap to be done immediately. The procedure which followed, marked a downward spiral of Olivier's condition until helplessly he sank into an abyss. He fell asleep.

I experienced a fitful sleep on the couch in Olivier's hospital room being startled and awakened around two in the morning by the Holy Spirit. I was told to gather from my husband all the names of the medications that Olivier had taken. The Lord showed me clearly as I went through a mental check list, which medication was compounding Olivier's illness.

This was my first clear indication of Olivier's true condition.

The Lord took me back to the night I gave Olivier the suppository from the pharmacist. I trembled with fear thinking I had administered a deadly drug to my grandson that could prove to be fatal. I had given him Diclofenac and his fever had gone down, but Olivier had felt shaky the next day. I found out from the Physicians' Desk Reference (PDR) that doctors at both PCH and Gleneagles in Kuala Lumpur had continued to administer this drug in the form of Voltaren although I had spoken to them about the reaction Olivier had the day he fell on the floor unable to get up without my and Rose's assistance.

The next morning Wednesday, April 1, after having that revelation, I duly reported my suspicions about the medicine to his team of doctors however; they blatantly disregarded what I said and apparently neither mentioned this at the daily reporting nor on his chart that he might have had an allergic reaction to Diclofenac. I had to repeat this story, which often fell upon deaf ears, throughout the duration of Olivier's hospital stay. No one took me seriously. In fact, as I previously mentioned he had been given Diclofenac both at Prince Court and Gleneagles.

Doctors ordered yet another MRI to be done immediately followed by a Computerized Axial Tomography (CAT) scan. A Magnetic Resonance Imaging (MRI) scan is a radiology technique that uses magnetism, radio waves, and a computer to produce images of body structures.

When compared to traditional X-Ray images, both MRI and CAT scans yield a much better degree of contrast between the various tissues of the body. Olivier had been given a CAT scan in KL after developing opsoclonus/myoclonus.

Miraculously, results were unchanged from previous tests done in Kuala Lumpur (KL).

Olivier's rapid health decline was very troubling for me as I sought to hear more from God. My physical strength was waning in contrast my spiritual was gaining momentum.

Paul's words from 2 Corinthians 12:10 New International Version (NIV) were at work in my life;

"For the sake of Christ, then, I am content with weaknesses, insults, hardships, persecutions, and calamities. For when I am weak, then I am strong."

On Thursday, April 2, the following evening, Rose, Olivier's nanny arrived in Singapore from Malaysia thus I had a chance to go to my friend's home for a good night's rest.

I was awakened by the Lord at exactly **5:34 a.m**. the next morning. I knew the time because my friend had a digital clock next to my bedside table and the digits were illuminated.

I quickly got up and dressed not wanting to be late getting to the hospital. While I sat downstairs waiting on my friend's husband to appear, (who so graciously agreed to drop me off at the hospital), the Holy Spirit flashed a scripture before my eyes and nudged me to read Mark 5:34. I was astonished as I recalled 5:34 were the exact numbers that had been illuminated on the digital clock when I woke up that morning! I felt the Holy Spirit was speaking to me in code. I quickly thumbed through my Bible to find the sacred words of the Lord that read,

Mark 5:34 Contemporary English Version (CEV):

"34 Jesus said to the woman, 'You are now well because of your faith. May God give you peace! You are healed, and you will no longer be in pain.'"

Mark 5:34 Amplified Bible (AMP)

"34 Then He said to her, 'Daughter, your faith [your personal trust and confidence] in Me has restored you to health; go in peace and be [permanently] healed from your suffering.'"

Mark 5:34 English Standard Version (ESV)

"34 And he said to her, 'Daughter, your faith has made you well; go in peace, and be healed of your disease.'"

I have chosen to quote this scripture in different versions in order to build your faith. For me, I knew instantly it was spiritual preparation for the task ahead! Much later, I realized this had been part of the verse that I had used in the theme of our Women's Conference the previous year! How marvelous of our Lord Jesus Christ, to take a verse of scripture, I had meditated on countless times and make it my reality!

Hebrews 4:12-13 (ESV)

"12 For the word of God is living and active, sharper than any two-edged sword, piercing to the division of soul and of spirit, of joints and of marrow, and discerning the thoughts and intentions of the heart. 13 And no creature is hidden from his sight, but all are naked and exposed to the eyes of him to whom we must give account."

In short, the Lord was saying to me, ***"Rhonda, your faith will make Olivier whole."***

This would be the pattern of speech the Lord chose to use with me throughout Olivier's ordeal and convalescence. Whether or not I had committed a scripture to memory was of no consequence to the Lord. He was gentle and patient; not overbearing or condemning. Yet He chose to reveal His Word to me in a miraculous fashion! Clear and concise leaving me with no other choice but to believe that it was He who was speaking to me! The Holy Spirit brought back to my memory how I had desired to be on a 'Word Fast' for Easter. And so I was.

In my conversation with the Lord, He spoke increasingly more and more through His Word until His Word became inseparable from Him. I finally understood the passage in:

John 1:1 ***"In the beginning was the Word and the Word was God and the Word was with God."***

You cannot separate God from His Word. When He speaks a Word, IT CANNOT return void but MUST accomplish his purpose. His Word separates bone and marrow, discerning the thoughts of man. The prophet Jeremiah said in 20:9;

"His word is in my heart like a fire, a fire shut up in my bones".

As unpleasant as the situation (Olivier's illness) was, nevertheless it was so refreshing to be in partnership with the Lord. To be graced with such a wonderful gift as to be able to talk with the Father daily and to hear HIM speak back to me! Simply incredible! To hear His voice SO clearly ringing through the ears of my SPIRIT! Surely; this must have been an indication of how Adam and Eve felt when the Lord walked in the cool of the garden and conversed with his first creation with no hindrances.

Whether my face shone as Moses did by being in the presence of "I AM" was irrelevant. What was certain was that I was hearing from God. For some reason other than I could discern, the Father had chosen to 'talk me through this ordeal' and I was more than willing to consent to His leading.

Believing for Olivier's healing hinged ONLY on God's spoken Word given to me in Mark 5:34. The Lord reminded me that this was the scripture from our Women's Conference last year, which I had temporarily forgotten. It had been hidden deep in my spirit and at the opportune time had surfaced as a revelation "Rhema" Word for Olivier's condition.

Rhema (ῥῆμα in Greek) literally means an "utterance" or "thing said" in Greek. It is a word that signifies the action of utterance [5].

Share Faith says the following about the Rhema Word:

"To newer Christians, the word rhema is completely unfamiliar. Long-term believers often speak of hearing the rhema word of God, and they consider it precious and something special enough to continually pursue."

In Greek, the word rhema means "an utterance." Therefore, the rhema word in Biblical terms refers to a portion of scripture that "speaks" to a believer. In most cases, a rhema word received while reading the Bible applies to a current situation or need. In essence, the rhema word is timely and extremely valuable in a Christian's walk with God.

In 2 Timothy 3:16, the Apostle Paul says that God inspired the writers of the Bible.

"All Scripture is given by inspiration of God, and is profitable for doctrine, for reproof, for correction, for instruction in righteousness, that the man of God may be complete, thoroughly equipped for every good work."

In the New International Version of the Bible, it says that Scripture is God-breathed. No matter the interpretation, the writers of the Bible put words to paper as the Holy Spirit instructed them.

With this understanding, Christians can count on the written words contained in the Bible to have deep and personal meaning to their lives. And it is the Holy Spirit who enlightens believers when reading a Scripture, with the goal of imparting wisdom, knowledge or understanding in order to have an immediate impact. This is a great promise of God; that He is with us when we read His word and He is able to make His words come alive in our hearts.

Though the Greek word Rhema does not appear in non-Greek Bibles, Matthew 4:4 is an excellent example of its importance.

"Man shall not live by bread alone, but by every word [rhema] that proceeds out of the mouth of God."

In John 6:63, Jesus confirmed this point when he said:

"The words [rhema] that I speak to you are spirit, and they are life."

Through daily reading of God's Word, which is referred to as the "logos," (logos), Christians will have knowledge of God and be able to memorize Scripture and to offer non-believers the truth that is written. But in addition to that, God wants to speak to His people and provide insight beyond human understanding. With the help of the Holy Spirit, portions of Scripture that were once words on a page will become rhema. They will have great significance and offer supernatural guidance, comfort, answers and assurances.

Intermittent rhema from Scripture is good, but daily rhema will guide a Christian's steps and move them toward greater understanding, revelation and joy[6].

Arriving at the hospital on that fateful Thursday morning, which was April the 2nd; things became increasingly clear that my faith indeed would be the deciding factor for Olivier's healing. This was huge for me and indeed weighed on my Spirituality. I knew that I could not afford to fail.

Olivier was non-responsive to the nurses and to his nanny, Rose, however; he moved his eyelids when I spoke to him but didn't open his eyes.

Due to Olivier's decreased consciousness and the long Easter weekend ahead, doctors recommended he be sent from the HD (High Dependency) Ward to ICU (Intensive Care Unit) where there would be 24 hour surveillance and he would be connected to life support.

As I didn't produce the expected dramatic response of worry that the neurologist expected, they repeated their plan enunciating each word until I responded favorably and confirmed that I understood. Indeed I was concerned but I refused to be worried.

At that particular time, I had been so grateful for the Word God had given me early that morning. It was His Word that sustained me as we gathered our things and moved to the ICU.

The ICU was different from the HD Ward. We were not allowed in his room 24-7 so Rose and I took turns going in. There was an ICU nurse who was in Olivier's room permanently. They had connected Olivier to life support paraphernalia and given him Keppra for suspected seizures and morphine for pain.

Keppra is an anti-epileptic drug, also called an anticonvulsant. It is used for the treatment of partial onset seizures[7]. Morphine is a narcotic pain reliever used to treat moderate to severe pain[8].

At this point, I would like to share scripture which will enable you understand better how God used His Word for Olivier's healing.

Firstly, it is important to note how God gave me peace in the midst of my storm. I obtained this peace through faith in God's Word but also due to the many prayers that were being prayed in Oasis, at my church, by Olivier's parents and their friends and our extended family and friends all over the world.

Isaiah 26: 3, 4 (ESV) says:

"You keep him in perfect peace whose mind is stayed on you, because he trusts in you. Trust in the LORD forever, for the LORD GOD is an everlasting rock."

The Message Bible says it in plain English verse 3:

"People with their minds set on you,
*** you keep completely whole,***
Steady on their feet,
*** because they keep at it and don't quit.***
Depend on GOD and keep at it
*** because in the LORD GOD you have a sure thing."***

The Expanded Bible reads in verse 3:

"You, LORD, give [preserve/keep in] true peace [complete peace; peace, peace] to those who depend on you whose mind is stayed on you; whose purpose is firm, because they trust you."

No matter which version of this scripture you read, you have the assurance from the Prince of Peace who is none other than Jesus Christ. Isaiah 9:6 (ESV) says:

"For to us a child is born, to us a son is given; and the government shall be upon his shoulder, and his name shall be called Wonderful Counselor, Mighty God, Everlasting Father, Prince of Peace."

It should be noted that I CHOSE to believe and trust in God. I chose NOT to trust in the doctor's words or prognosis. In return, because of the grace of God, I received an extraordinary gift of peace.

The fruit of the Spirit includes a peace that goes beyond that of salvation. It is a sweet relationship. We are called to His presence (Ephesians 2:11-18) and called to be confident in that presence (Hebrews 4:16) because we are His friends (John 15:15). As I've already stated in Isaiah 26:3, 4 (ESV), which states:

"You keep him in perfect peace whose mind is stayed on you, because he trusts in you. Trust in the LORD forever, for the LORD GOD is an everlasting rock."

God's peace transcends earthly matters, as Philippians 4:4-7 illustrates. Believers are to be ***"anxious for nothing,"*** for God promises to ***"guard your hearts and minds."*** It is a peace ***"which transcends all understanding"***; that is, to the worldly mind, such peace is incomprehensible. Its source is the Holy Spirit of God, whom the world neither sees nor knows (John 14:17).

The Spirit-filled Christian should possess a peace that is abundant and fully accessible in every situation (reference John 14:27). The alternative to being filled with the Spirit and His peace is to be filled with alarm, gloom and doubt. To allow dread or foreboding to take you captive! Why not allow the Holy Spirit to take the reins of your life allowing Him to work in you producing the fruit of patience and perseverance for the glory of the Father?

Chapter 6

Capable Doctors

We had very capable doctors in every sense of the word. However, in Olivier's case, we needed a divine intervention from God. Olivier had one of the best team of doctors and nurses I have ever known. The Lord uses doctors to bring about His purpose.

Certainly, one of my very best friends is a doctor, Dr. Yemisi-Adeyemi-Bero. She specializes in IVF (In Vitro Fertilization), this refers to the fertilization of eggs by sperm outside the body. When she meets with her clients, she lets them know up front that she is a Christian and that she depends upon God for help in each case presented to her. She prays before or during each consultation.

I know doctors have been given their knowledge. The Message Bible says it like this in Daniel 2:21a
"He changes the seasons and guides history, He raises up kings and also brings them down; he provides both intelligence and discernment,"

Jesus is the Great Physician: Twice in scripture He referred to himself as a "physician" or "doctor," once in the sense of "spiritual healer" and once in the sense of "physical healer."

Jesus as Spiritual Healer: His opponents once attacked Him for having unsavory characters among His disciples. Jesus reminded them in Mark 2:17 that
"It is not the healthy who need a doctor, but the sick. I have not come to call the righteous, but sinners."

Jesus as Physical Healer: When Jesus gave his first sermon in his hometown synagogue of Nazareth (Luke 4:23), He challenged them:
"Surely you will quote this proverb to me: 'Physician, heal yourself'! Do here in your hometown what we have heard that you did in Capernaum."

Furthermore, the Bible talks about:

"How God anointed Jesus of Nazareth with the Holy Spirit and with power. He went about doing good and healing all who were oppressed by the devil, for God was with him." (Acts 10:38 (ESV).

We have learned from these scriptures that Jesus is The Great Physician. But NOT only that, He went around **DOING GOOD** and healing **ALL** who were oppressed by the devil for God was with Him! I reasoned that when God is for you, then WHO can be against you? He also gives wisdom and knowledge to doctors. God has commissioned all who are His followers to lay hands on the sick and they shall recover. This is called the "Great Commission." We can find this in:

Mark 16:15-20, The Message (MSG)

"14-16 Still later, as the Eleven were eating supper, he appeared and took them to task most severely for their stubborn unbelief, refusing to believe those who had seen him raised up. Then he said, 'Go into the world. Go everywhere and announce the Message of God's good news to one and all. Whoever believes and is baptized is saved; whoever refuses to believe is damned.
17-18 These are some of the signs that will accompany believers: 'They will throw out demons in my name, they will speak in new tongues, they will take snakes in their hands, they will drink poison and not be hurt, they will lay hands on the sick and make them well'.
19-20 Then the Master Jesus, after briefing them, was taken up to heaven, and he sat down beside God in the place of honor. And the disciples went everywhere preaching, the Master working right with them, validating the Message with indisputable evidence."

Believers, we can be assured of this one thing. That Jesus of Nazareth has intended that we continue His work. He came to destroy the works of the devil. Sickness and death are from the enemy. God would have us believe, have faith and continue His work here on earth. He said in John 14:12 that we would even do greater works than He! We can lay hands on our Loved Ones and watch them recover. In GOD'S WORD Translation:
"I can guarantee this truth: Those who believe in me will do the things that I am doing. They will do even greater things because I am going to the Father".

Chapter 7

A Risk of Faith

Let us look at Mark 5:21-43 in the Message Bible. Verse 34 was the crux of the issue. The numbers that were on the clock's dial at my friend's house were 5:34. These numbers represented the verse that I believe the Holy Spirit dropped in my spirit on the second day in Singapore.

For context, let's begin to read from verse 21-24:

"After Jesus crossed over by boat, a large crowd met him at the seaside. One of the meeting-place leaders named Jairus came. When he saw Jesus, he fell to his knees, beside himself as he begged, 'My dear daughter is at death's door. Come and lay hands on her so she will get well and live.' Jesus went with him, the whole crowd tagging along, pushing and jostling him.

25-29 A woman who had suffered a condition of hemorrhaging for twelve years—a long succession of physicians had treated her, and treated her badly, taking all her money and leaving her worse off than before—had heard about Jesus. She slipped in from behind and touched his robe. She was thinking to herself, 'If I can put a finger on his robe, I can get well.' The moment she did it, the flow of blood dried up. She could feel the change and knew her plague was over and done with.

30 At the same moment, Jesus felt energy discharging from him. He turned around to the crowd and asked, 'Who touched my robe?'

31 His disciples said, 'What are you talking about? With this crowd pushing and jostling you, you're asking, 'Who touched me? Dozens have touched you!'

32-33 But he went on asking, looking around to see who had done it. The woman, knowing what had happened, knowing she was the one, stepped up in fear and trembling, knelt before him, and gave him the whole story.

34 Jesus said to her, 'Daughter, you took a risk of faith, and now you're healed and whole. Live well, live blessed! Be healed of your plague.'

35 While he was still talking, some people came from the leader's house and told him, 'Your daughter is dead. Why bother the Teacher anymore?'

36 Jesus overheard what they were talking about and said to the leader, 'Don't listen to them; just trust me.'

37-40 He permitted no one to go in with him except Peter, James, and John. They entered the leader's house and pushed their way through the gossips looking for a story and neighbors bringing in casseroles. Jesus was abrupt: 'Why all this busybody grief and gossip? This child isn't dead; she's sleeping.' Provoked to sarcasm, they told him he didn't know what he was talking about.

40-43 But when he had sent them all out, he took the child's father and mother, along with his companions, and entered the child's room. He clasped the girl's hand and said, 'Talitha koum,' which means, 'Little girl, get up.' At that, she was up and walking around! This girl was twelve years of age. They, of course, were all beside themselves with joy. He gave them strict orders that no one was to know what had taken place in that room. Then he said, 'Give her something to eat.'"

From Mark 5: 25-43 above, the Lord unfolded Olivier's illness to me; Mark 5:26 speaks of a woman who had suffered a condition of hemorrhaging for twelve years--a long succession of physicians had treated her, and treated her badly, taking all her money leaving her worse off than before--but she had heard about Jesus.

The woman with the issue of blood had suffered a great deal under the care of many doctors and had spent all she had yet instead of getting better she grew worse. The Lord showed me that Olivier was suffering from effects of the medication. He had been diagnosed rightly with Mycoplasma Pneumonia but he had suffered adverse effects and a severe reaction to Diclofenac, the suppository recommended by the pharmacist. Diclofenac had assisted in lowering Olivier's fever and was subsequently prescribed by both Prince Court and Gleneagles but did not agree with Olivier's body.

Let me pause for a moment to explain my view of pharmaceutical companies. Once more, I am a nurse and have great respect for doctors. So I am NOT despising doctors or the medical field. I am simply relating to you what happened to my grandson in this particular situation and what the Spirit of the Lord said to me.

Numbers 21:8-9 (NIV) tells the story of the Israelites when they rebelled against God. They travelled from Mt Hor towards Edom. The people grew impatient on the way and spoke against God and against Moses protesting, 'Why have you brought us up out of Egypt to die in the wilderness? There is no bread, there is no water! And we detest this miserable food' (manna from heaven). Mind you they had been delivered from Egypt by the hand of God, come through the Red Sea and seen the deliverance of God on several occasions!

"And the Lord said unto Moses, make thee a fiery serpent, and set it upon a pole, and it shall come to pass, that every one that is bitten, when he looketh upon it shall live. And Moses made a serpent of brass, and put it upon a pole, and came to pass, that if a serpent had bitten any man, when he beheld the serpent of brass, he lived."

God wanted his people to have a better understanding of his plan for them. All over the world, the figure of a serpent wrapped around a pole is the accepted logo for the medical profession. Here in Holland where I now live, there is a hospital that depicts this model accurately.

Literally, in that scripture, God was telling his people 'If you're bitten by a venomous snake, don't fret the poison, rather lift your eyes to the bronze serpent and the poison will be neutralized.'

I believe doctors are saying by that logo is, 'We treat, but God heals. Keep your eyes on God'. When doctors come to their wits end or when they declare a case hopeless, God takes over.

What is the Word of God telling you here? See John 3:14-15 (NIV)

"And as Moses lifted the serpent in the wilderness even so must the Son of man be lifted up. That whosoever believeth in him should not perish but have eternal life."

If God of the Old Testament brought up three million Jews from Egypt who lived in the desert for 40 years and none were sick then why would the God of the New Testament NOT heal His people! He says He is the Lord who healeth thee! In Isaiah 53:5 He took 39 stripes on His back for your sickness. In a sermon by Dr. Dale A Robbins, he believes in medical science every sickness falls under a category of 39! This is NO coincidence!

When drugs are tested, most of the time they are not tested on thousands of people, but a select few. Sometimes drugs are tested on animals, rats or monkeys. In this case, Diclofenac had been tested on 1000 people and as a result adverse effects have not been widely reported.

There are contraindications that are given and it may say on the notice 'In rare cases you may have this occurrence'. Well guess what, when you go down the list on the rare side of Diclofenac Olivier had almost EVERY SYMPTOM!

Diclofenac is a nonsteroidal anti-inflammatory drug (NSAID). This medicine works by reducing substances in the body that cause pain and inflammation. Diclofenac is used to treat mild to moderate pain, or signs and symptoms of osteoarthritis or rheumatoid arthritis[9].

Olivier experienced the majority of these overdose symptoms from day one! (See appendix for further reference).

The Lord impressed upon me to request that the Life Support be removed because many of the medications had induced his present state and only then would he come back to us. My job was to convince the doctors!

My key verse kept coming back to me from Mark 5:34;

"Jesus said to her, 'Daughter, your faith has healed you. Go in peace and be freed from your suffering.'"

Chapter 8

A Word on Faith

Hebrews 11:1 Living Bible:

"What is faith? It is the confident assurance that something we want is going to happen. It is the certainty that what we hope for is waiting for us, even though we cannot see it up ahead."

I knew I would have to possess unshakeable faith for Olivier's healing. I needed to believe and not doubt.

Clement could be a bit of a sceptic but I knew I had to get him to believe. Rose was not a regular church goer and I was unsure of where she stood in her faith due to the fact that she was a non-practicing Catholic. Nevertheless, I knew I had to get both Clement and Rose to have faith and believe along with me for Olivier's miracle.

Without their assistance, I would not be able to convince the doctors nor the nurses. Unless they believed that I was truly hearing from God, I might be regarded as being a *deranged lunatic*.

Again, the Lord's Word showed me how to convince them in Mark 5:37 where Jesus permitted only his closest companions to go in with him for the healing of Jarius's daughter. Jesus was radical. He pushed past all the fanfare, weeping and nonsense which might interfere with the girl's parents believing in Him. He took only Peter, James, John and the child's parents inside the room with Him and sent everyone else away!

Jesus knew firsthand how **doubt and unbelief** could wreak havoc in the things pertaining to faith. Therefore He permitted no doubters in the room with him.

After such a miraculous occurrence He would leave and go into his own home town to face grave disappointment because of their lack of faith. In Mark 6:5 (NIV), Jesus encountered severe doubt in His own home town and was unable to perform miracles! Look what the scripture tells us:

Mark 6:5-6 (NIV):

"He could not do any miracles there, except lay his hands on a few sick people and heal them. He was amazed at their lack of faith."

His relatives and friends were busy gossiping about the fact that He was a carpenter's son and not a learned man. They marveled at and questioned His wisdom.

Jesus responded,

"A prophet is not without honor except in his own town, among his relatives and in his own home."

> *But He brings His Kingdom into the realm of the earth and that is what we are commissioned to do.*

I knew this to be so. Nevertheless, I successfully rallied Clement and Rose's support. Then although Alesea and Carmelo were not physically in Singapore, they were Olivier's parents therefore I still had to convince them to believe that God would heal Olivier despite the doctor's prognosis. Alesea persevered in persuading her husband to trust in God's Word.

In Mark 5:39 (MSG) Jesus was abrupt when he arrived in Jarius home. He put out all the mourners. He only took his closest companions and the parents inside the room were the child lay. It reads:

Jesus was abrupt. "Why all this busybody grief and gossip? This child isn't dead; she's sleeping.' Provoked to sarcasm, they told him he didn't know what he was talking about."

I believe He said this in order to build the faith of the parents and the disciples. Jesus was radical!

Olivier's doctors recognized that Olivier was in a decreased state of consciousness but never uttered the word coma. I sincerely believe that God did not allow the neurologists to use this term as God's purpose had been revealed to me through his Word.

Above we read how Jesus told the people Jarius' child was NOT dead but sleeping. Obviously all around they knew that she was clinically dead. It should be noted that Jesus does not speak as the world does. But He brings His Kingdom into the realm of the earth and that is what we are commissioned to do.

In the Lord's Prayer, we pray "your kingdom come your will be done on earth as it is in heaven" (reference The Lord's Prayer in Matthew 6:10 NIV). The Bible says there is no death in heaven; therefore, we need to bring that reality to earth.

It also says in Isaiah 55:9 (NIV) *"As the heavens are higher than the earth, so are my ways higher than your ways and my thoughts than your thoughts."*

My task was to convince the doctors about Olivier's case. I had to reassure them that he was not in a coma (only a medical induced one). I needed to let them know that he would not die and that he was only sleeping! After all he had not slept for three days.

This spiritual truth took root in my life producing fruit in Clement and Rose's lives. They also chose to believe the Word of God ignoring the clinical symptoms before their very eyes. A miracle was brewing under the surface. We just needed to take hold and make it our reality. Now this is faith!

The Word became life and truth for Rose. She actually began to believe God. So much so, she rededicated her life to the Lord and started attending church with me while in Singapore and continued once back in KL!

With Rose and Clement as my allies, I had renewed determination to administer and devour the Word that had been spoken to me. The doctors scorned me and questioned her several times about my sanity and Olivier's condition. They would touch me lightly me on my back in empathy of my grandson's case! But I wasn't having any of their 'empathy!' I set my face like flint to preserve his life!

Chapter 9

<u>Easter Eve</u>

Each day, since arriving in Singapore, my prayer partner and dear friend, Carol, had inquired in regards to Olivier's condition and I wasn't giving her much information to go on. Most of my texts to her were vague. My go to phrase became: "It is well". I did not want to alarm anyone, most of all the people who were praying for Olivier. Once a day prayer requests that were inspired by the Holy Spirit and led by my walking buddy would be sent out to the ladies Bible Study. Here is one of the first ones to be sent out by Carol.

Dear Sisters,

I'm sending out a request for Urgent prayer for Olivier, Rhonda's grandson who has been in and out of the hospital for the past two weeks. He has been diagnosed with Mycoplasma Pneumoniae which is quite common in children.

They are going to Singapore to see a top pediatrician and receive the best possible care. Please pray:

1. Safe, rapid, trouble free travels to Singapore.
2. Speedy and complete recovery for Olivier.
3. Wisdom for doctor's and medical staff
4. Good health and peace and rest for Rhonda (Ko Ko) and Clement (Grand Pa)
5. Peace and comfort for Olivier's parents back home in the USA

I feel in my Spirit that this is a full on attack of the enemy! Please read Ephesians 6 and keep the armor on and please cover Rhonda and family in prayer without ceasing. Thessalonians 5:17
If you feel called to fast and pray please do what the Lord is calling you to do and He will strengthen you.

In His service,

Carol

I will be forever grateful for my friend's love, dedication and determination to keep the prayer wheel turning!

My mindset had to be changed radically in order to receive this miracle from God! My communication with the outside world was limited. My husband censored my calls and responded on my behalf to many that were calling who were interested in our grandson's case. I kept my mind unpolluted from doubt and unbelief. It would take a miracle to bring Olivier back but I knew the God I served was a miracle worker and NOTHING was impossible with Him!

A major decision had to be made at one point, whether to transfer Olivier to the USA by private plane. This would cost hundreds of thousands of dollars.

Clement and the family relied on me as the spiritual guru throughout Olivier's illness. What I said, they knew that God was saying because I spoke like God, meaning, I spoke His word. I spoke in faith!

As I've said earlier, Rose and I would take turns at Olivier's bedside and once Clement brought my jogging shoes and clothes from KL, I started taking faith walks, talking out loud to God and declaring His Word over Olivier's life. This could not be done inside the hospital. So I would walk and walk, unaware of my pace and oblivious to the scorching heat outside.

But when I was told about the important decision we had to make on whether or not to evacuate to the USA, I didn't have time to walk at all. I simply went downstairs to the children's inside covered play-ground. The joyful noise of the children surrounding me contrasted my grandson's reality. Under normal circumstances, I would not have been able to think or pray in such chaos and noise, yet on this occasion, the voice of the Lord pierced through the boisterous sounds and sights. My ears had been attuned to listen to the voice of the Master.

Satan began to point out to me children being brought into the hospital (by their parents or relatives) lying lethargic in wheelchairs---merely 'vegetables'. I was imagining Olivier spending the rest of his life in that condition in diapers, drooling and unable to come back to us whole.

"Should Olivier be sent to the USA for better health care?" I inquired of the Lord. Clement had said emphatically, "No, let's rely on the Word of God," when I had spoken to him just a few minutes earlier. The Word of God came speedily to me!

"Affliction shall not arise a second time" Nahum 1:9 (NIV).

That was the scripture that flashed in my mind. It was not one I had memorized but from time to time on Wednesday nights, our Senior Pastor in KL would quote this scripture.

I didn't even have it highlighted in my Bible, but now I do. So a major decision such as whether to transfer Olivier to the USA for better health-care or leave him in Singapore was made *merely* on the Word of God. The Word of God was alive and active to me! I depended upon God's Word for Olivier's complete healing. Now that is faith in action!

Chapter 10

<u>The Big Turn Around</u>

The 'Big Turn Around' occurred on Sunday April 5, 2015, Easter morning and what a glorious morning it was! It was no coincidence that on the day Christians around the world celebrated the Resurrection of Jesus Christ, we were steadfast in faith believing the same thing for Olivier.

Clement and I had attended a beautiful Good Friday service at our host family's church. We were so thankful for their hospitality. Their support was priceless during this season of our lives.

Although, I wanted to go back to their Church for Easter Sunday, my husband felt it crucial we remain at the hospital near Olivier's bedside. Clements's faith had started to be built up. He was certain God's power would be manifested on this Easter Sunday.

In my 'faith walks' I often took each morning, I passed a church across the street from the hospital. During these walks, I would pray, talk to the Lord and listen. Since Clement felt we should remain at the hospital, I decided to attend a worship service there.

We were still in ICU where there was 24 hour surveillance nevertheless we tended not to both leave Olivier's bedside unless one of us was present. It is a medical fact that when people seem to be unconscious, they can still hear and their senses are still intact. We wanted Olivier to feel the love of his family around him and hear our voices. It was common for us to speak to him throughout the day whether there was a response from him or not. I felt it was comforting for him.

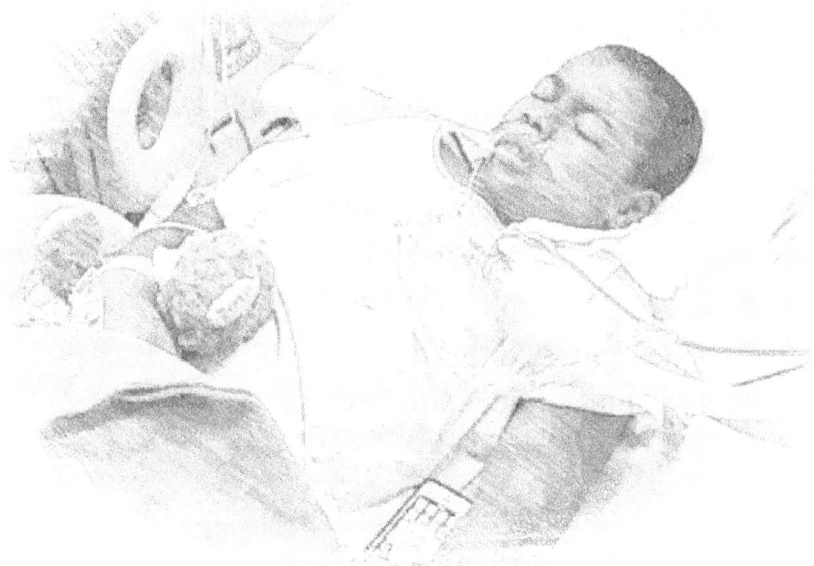

I slipped out of the room, leaving Clement to keep watch over Olivier. Rose stayed behind in the waiting area. ICU had many critical cases that could cause one to lose ALL faith and hope. While Olivier was in ICU, Clement took time out to comfort and encourage other parents who were in similar situations as ours.

But not I, all of my time spent in the ICU, I mainly kept vigil over 'my ward'. There was no time to pray for others or counsel others. My time and energy were spent for my grandson. I love people and have a desire to reach out to them, but on this occasion, 'my assignment' only involved my grandson. My focus and desire was to see Olivier totally well. It was a focused desire but it was my 'mission impossible'.

"*With God all things are possible to he who believes!*" Mark 9:23

I walked passed all of the dismal cases in the hospital gladly rushing into the sunlight of Sunday morning Resurrection day. Hope sprung forth and joined with my faith. Upon arrival in the sanctuary of the church, I met with an elderly Indian saint who happened to be a retired Pastor. She spoke perfect English and welcomed me wholeheartedly. She questioned me about where I was coming from and why I was there. After my explanation, she readily offered to pray for Olivier.

The Bible talks about a powerful prayer of agreement in Matthew 18:18-20 and this is what we did right there in the empty sanctuary.

After our prayer, people began trickling in, there was to be a dual English and Tamil Service and I was excited that I had made it just in time. My phone rang. It was Clement telling me the doctors were there. I heard the urgency in his voice and knew I had to return. I left the church, promising the elderly saint I would return shortly.

I met with Olivier's neurologists including the ICU doctors and also his regular neurologist, who had been with us since we arrived at the hospital. I spoke with them matter-of-factly and requested they remove the breathing tube as well as stop administering Keppra for seizures and morphine for pain.

Christianity is relational.

This wasn't the first time I had made this request, but this time I was firm and after my prayer with the retired Pastor, I hoped they would respect our wishes. To my sheer amazement they agreed! I trusted God and knew it would be good! It was God's timing.

I would like to create a parenthesis here. As you might be thinking, "Why would I choose to return to church instead of staying by Olivier's bedside and to watch God accomplish His Word?"

First I would like to point out the importance of meeting with believers as the Lord admonishes in the following scripture:

Hebrews 10:25 (NJV) states ***"Not forsaking the assembling of ourselves together, as the manner of some is; but exhorting one another; and so much the more, as ye see the day approaching."***

There are those of us who believe we can simply watch Christian television or tune in to teaching on the internet and this suffices in establishing a Christian rapport with the Lord. Maybe with the Lord, but what about with your brethren?

Christianity is relational. It's all about relationship with others. Relationship with God is vertical but with your fellowman horizontal. I chuckle in remembrance of my randomly choosing Hebrews 10:25 in a scripture basket while in a French Church in Paris. A friend and I attended New Year Eve's service one year and the clergy had carefully folded scriptures for parishioners to choose from. These scriptures were meant to give them direction for the coming year. I loved this method as I had learned to do this with my Doctor friend I mentioned earlier. She did this during Women Conferences as a fun activity.

However; I was puzzled why the Lord had given me that particular Word in 2011. The Lord knew that from my father's upbringing we were taught to reverence the Sabbath. At Double Portion Church where I had attended during my adult life, the Pastor honed in the same teaching. Now in a small Assembly in France I was getting the same Word! It was a reminder to me that no matter what occurred I needed to stay connected to the Saints and to the Church. Much unfolded in that following year that caused Hebrews 10:25 to become my 'sacred bread'.

> *There is a difference between waiting on God and waiting in God.*

The second thing I would like to point out is the difference between waiting in God and waiting ON God. The Bible says in Isaiah 40:31 "***But they that wait upon the Lord shall renew their strength; they shall mount up with wings as eagles; they shall run, and not be weary; and they shall walk, and not faint***. I was waiting in God but needed to charge up my faith! This required being in the presence of God and releasing my faith enabling me to embrace the umbrella of his protection previously promised through his rainbow covenant. I simply needed to activate my faith to believe.

Spiritual waiting on God denotes a need for intercession and prayer. When God speaks a Word, the interval between when He speaks and when He accomplishes His Word is when you need to be praying.

In 1 Kings 18:41-46 (NIV) Elijah had declared a famine in the land and King Ahab was angry because the entire nation was suffering. Merely at the Word of Elijah, there was neither rain nor dew on the earth for three and a half years! We are men and women just like Elijah and we can also speak and it will happen!

"And Elijah said to Ahab, 'Go, eat and drink, for there is the sound of a heavy rain.' So Ahab went off to eat and drink, but Elijah climbed to the top of Carmel, bent down to the ground and put his face between his knees.

'Go and look toward the sea,' he told his servant. And he went up and looked.

'There is nothing there,' he said.

Seven times Elijah said, 'Go back.'

The seventh time the servant reported, 'A cloud as small as a man's hand is rising from the sea.'

So Elijah said, 'Go and tell Ahab, Hitch up your chariot and go down before the rain stops you.'

Meanwhile, the sky grew black with clouds, the wind rose, a heavy rain started falling and Ahab rode off to Jezreel. The power of the Lord came on Elijah and, tucking his cloak into his belt, he ran ahead of Ahab all the way to Jezreel."

Do you see what Elijah did? He spoke the Word of God to Ahab in Faith. He heard in the Spirit rain but there was NO physical manifestation! This defies nature therefore you cannot use your cognitive sense in the things of God.

> *But our God is the ultimate Pay Master and we will reap the benefits of our diligence in prayer!*

The man of God had to go to the mountain with his servant and bend his knees to pray for the manifestation of his Word! Intercession for others is a tedious and sometimes 'thankless job' as it is done in secret. Most people see the manifestation of God's work and have NO idea what faith was required to produce it! But our God is the ultimate Pay Master and we will reap the benefits of our diligence in prayer!

It is interesting that Elijah sent his servant to look for a cloud and it was only seen the 7th time after Elijah prayed! Seven is the number of completion and also will play an important part in Olivier's healing.

The sign of a small cloud for Elijah was enough to know that God was now acting on Elijah's spoken word! He knew that a mighty rain would follow so this old prophet ran a race in the power of God, galloping way ahead of the king's chariots and arriving at destination on feet before the rain began. Now that was divine speed!

This is why I chose to leave Clement in ICU while I went back to the English service and remain in God's presence. It was imperative that I pray and hear the Word of God that would increase my faith. This time Rose tagged along with me. I don't ever recall her having gone to church in KL.

The service turned out to be in English and Tamil. Tamil is the language that many Indians speak in that area. It was a quiet meeting but I felt the Spirit of God in everything they did. A wonderful Indian lady who sat on the pew next to me decided to translate most of the sermon for me!

I was pleasantly surprised that she chose to do this as the service was not entirely in English as we had expected it to be. The Pastor spoke some of the message in English but the majority was in Tamil. Rose and I were the only English speakers attending therefore there wasn't such a great need to speak only in English. Again, God's provision of a translator was such a blessing and exactly what we needed!

Chapter 11

Talitha Koum – Arise!

"He (Jesus) clasped the girl's hand and said, 'Talitha koum,' which means, 'Little girl, get up.'" Mark 5:41 (NIV)

I returned to the hospital totally refreshed; my faith was at a heightened state to believe God. Arriving back in ICU from the church service, I had faith to believe that Olivier would rise again. I knew that he would see, walk and talk soon. It was just a matter of time.

I saw that the doctors had decreased the oxygen level to zero but left in the breathing tube as a measure of support. They wanted to be cautious. The Keppra which had been given as a precautionary measure was discontinued as well as the morphine.

I relieved Clement of his bedside duty allowing him to go and grab some lunch. Rose remained in the waiting room since only one person at a time was allowed in ICU.

While I sat at Olivier's bedside on Easter Day believing God that he was healed, I heard the Spirit of the Lord say,

"Woman of God, do you believe?"

I looked at his lifeless, body and this song came to me;

"I believe, yes I receive it. My healing Lord, I believe, yes I receive it. I'm delivered".

I sang this song in Olivier's ear, took anointing oil, anointed him and breathed on him according to Ezekial chapter 37 when the prophet was asked by God to speak life to the army of dry bones. And so I began to speak life to Olivier's lifeless body! I sang the song as if it were Olivier singing it.

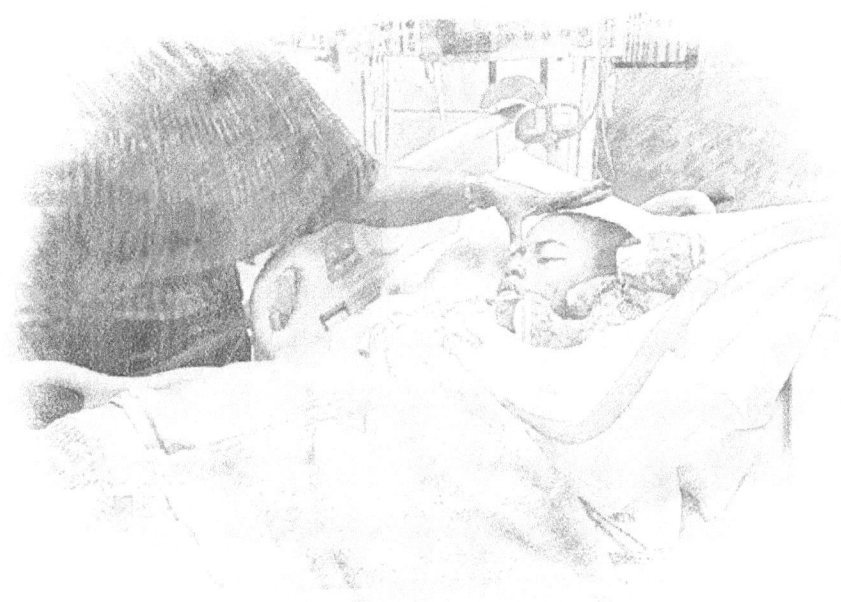

I stood in the gap and prayed. I believed in his stead, standing in the gap on his behalf.

As I ministered over Olivier's seemingly lifeless body, doctors and nurses were entering in and out of the room, but they respected my prayers and didn't interfere.

After Olivier's oxygen had been reduced, the doctors discovered he was breathing on his own! The nurses would suction Olivier several times a day as the saliva and secretions would run down his cheeks. Suctioning prevented him from choking or drowning in his own saliva.

That afternoon when I finished praying the nurses came in to perform their care as they usually would. But this time while suctioning Olivier, he began to cough! This was the first time this had ever happened and the first sign of life since arriving in ICU!

I spoke in the previous chapter how Elijah had prayed 7 times before seeing a manifestation of a miracle. When his servant reported seeing a cloud the size of a man's hand, this meant to the man of God, a mighty downpour was on the way and he ran for cover! Just as the tiny cloud was a sign for Elijah, the coughing was a sign for me! It clearly indicated to me that Olivier was alive and well and on his way back to us on Easter Sunday! On the day Christians celebrated the resurrection of our Lord, my grandson also was being resurrected by God!

The nurses were amazed at this change of events. After that, he started moving his eyes but not opening them. I started communicating with him right away. The doctors were doubtful of my means of communication and warned me not to get my hopes up. The doctors cautioned that one never knows what state the brain is in coming from a state of unconsciousness. This had been the 5th day. They advised that the recovery stage might take up to six months!

The emergency room doctors questioned Rose on the reliability of my report of his progress assuming that Olivier's movements were involuntary and not meaningful. But for Clement and I, these signs were enough for us to trust our God given instincts. We reasoned if God had been able to speak and bring this change about then surely He would complete the recovery in Olivier! We were MORE than convinced! We were certain!

Clement drove back to KL from Singapore, armed with the knowledge and proof that Olivier would be fine. Rose and I remained with Olivier at the hospital.

Chapter 12

Olivier's resurrection

Olivier's healing for me, in the Spirit, was instantaneous but in the natural, gradual. As the effects of the medication wore off, just as God predicted, his conscious level returned. First eye twitching, fluttering, then movement in his legs, then opening his eyes but he could not speak nor walk. In fact, most of his communication was done through violent movement of his legs and I knew just how frustrated he was becoming.

Olivier opening his eyes

When he was little and couldn't express himself, he would do the same. His Mom used to tell him when he got upset: "Olivier, don't internalize your anger but use your words".

But now, no words would come. Not even a sound! This state did NOT deter me in the least. I held firm to the Word of God and kept speaking, praying and believing God.

In the case of the little girl that Jesus resurrected from the dead in Mark 5:43, he says to her parents after she was brought back to life:

"Then he said, give her something to eat. "When the damsel was ill and resurrected, Jesus said "*give her something to eat.*"

This food would rally up the strength needed for her complete rehabilitation and so it would be with Olivier.

As I previously stated, Olivier lived with us in Bordeaux, France when he was 12 months old. At this time my French friends were amazed Olivier could hold a real fork and spoon correctly and could finish an adult bowl of spaghetti. He has always had a hearty appetite. He had been sick for almost a month now and hadn't had real food for that length of time. It was about time he had some tasty food to eat.

The next day, April 6, 2015, Olivier was moved from 24 hour surveillance to an open room in ICU with other patients. I felt that our victory was half way won when he opened his eyes! Oh, what a glorious day that was for me! He was able to follow me with his eyes and blink vigorously communicating to me his frustration in his inability to move or get up. It was as if he had awakened from a long sleep. I quickly summoned for the doctor to come who checked his pupils and eye movement. There was no more opsoclonus present!

Later on, Olivier was moved back up to the High Dependency Ward (HD). This was the first floor we were placed on when we arrived in Singapore.

Shortly after arriving on HD, a physical therapist came in to sit Olivier up with his legs dangling on the side of the bed. Oliver still didn't have complete use of his arms. I could just tell how frustrated he was, having to get up! I helped with this process while he fought to lie back down on the bed. His upper body went limp, but I held him up by standing in front facing him and holding his back up with my hands supporting him.

I was glad that this petite tenacious physical therapist was as determined as I was to see progress. She paid no attention to Olivier's protests. I don't think she realized he had just gotten to the ward and she certainly didn't realize the journey he had been on!

After the physical therapist left, there was a succession of rehabilitation personnel coming in and out. I was glad things were happening so fast. The speech therapist arrived to find me reading to Olivier to stimulate his brain. Olivier still exchanged communication with me by blinking his eyes. The speech therapist carried with her a series of tools to assist patients in Olivier's predicament to communicate. She was curious about my means of communication with him and encouraged me to stick to yes and no 'blinks' of his eyes to ensure that Olivier understood what I was saying. I glared at her. I was there at this child's birth and took care of him from 12 months to 18 months and again when he was four years old. I knew his personality inside out and I knew that he was not eager to respond to her method of learning, because he was fully present.

I put the fun book down and read from the Bible by his bedside and prayed over him. I also brought in other books to read to him. Olivier had been an avid reader and listened intently as I narrated the stories. His facial expressions let me know he fully understood everything that was going on. But the doctors were still not convinced. Their training dictated their reasoning. The brain was a complicated organ. They didn't want to exaggerate his progress and I fully understood their hesitation.

When Olivier had arrived in KL in September 2014 at the start of the school year, I had encouraged him to practice his handwriting. Together we wrote a short story and 'published' it. The extent of our publishing was to have him do the illustrations, have the pages laminated and the copy put together in book form. We distributed one to his teacher, one to his parents in the USA and retained one copy for ourselves. It was dedicated to his sister, Sanaa, and properly illustrated with pictures drawn by him. Olivier loved reading!

The speech therapist was unsure of his level of reading as well as to what extent his brain was functioning. However, by the end of the next session, she would become our greatest ally and most valuable player on the medical team! She would be the first one to validate what I had been telling the doctors all along; Olivier was perfectly normal and his brain intact!

The speech therapist first brought pictures for kindergarten reading level such as 'This is a house'. Olivier was reluctant to cooperate as he felt insulted. His noncompliance caused the therapist to wrongly assume, as the doctors did, that Olivier's brain was still not functioning to full capacity.

After the therapist left, I explained to Olivier this was part of the process. His participation in these activities would help the medical team comprised of doctors, physical therapists and other workers to assess him properly. I also told him that I knew he was hungry and wanted to eat. But before doing this, the therapist would need to access his swallowing mechanism. They wanted to be sure he would not choke. He would need to cooperate with the speech therapist in order to do that. He concurred by nodding his head.

The next day, Thursday April 9, 2015, Rose had been sitting at Olivier's bedside when the speech therapist came with an even more complicated chart which was a system of communication designed to assist patients who were unable to speak. I gave Rose a break while I watched the therapist work with Olivier. She was surprised how quickly he mastered it! In fact, she was so shocked that she left it in Olivier's room for us to use ---to my chagrin! The system of communication was so difficult and confusing for me to use to communicate with Olivier. I preferred our usual manner.

The therapist mentioned that none of her other patients including adults were able to comprehend the system. She had never really used it with a client up until now. I could certainly understand why! The method was extremely complex yet Olivier understood! This was a major breakthrough for us. Now she would be able to relay this information to the doctor. She wrote in Olivier's chart the progress she saw in him. She noted his thought pattern was intact! The doctors still assumed our communication was random.

Two days later, Saturday, April 11, we were moved to room 7 on a normal ward. It would take several pages to explain and demonstrate the signification of the number 7 in scripture but I will simply explain pertinent information for your complete understanding of God's faithfulness.

> *Notice the 7 on Olivier's door signifying completion. Could the leaf be symbolic of an Olive leaf indicating life? Release the Dove….*

From the Seven days of Creation to the Seven Seals of Revelation, Scripture is saturated with the number seven [10]. I'll begin with the Hebrew word for seven which is שׁבע (Sheva). Sheva carries three fundamental meanings: full, complete, oath and to swear. God marked the Bible with the number seven because I believe it is His Oath, His Promise and His Covenant!

God laid the foundation of its meaning when He introduced this number in the context of His finished work of creation which we can find in Genesis 2:2;

"And on the seventh day God ended his work which he had made; and he rested on the seventh day from all his work which he had made. And God blessed the seventh day, and sanctified it: because that in it he had rested from all his work which God created and made".

Seven is also the number of victory in the Bible as well as the number which signifies completion. Joshua had the Israelites walk around the walls of Jericho and when they shouted the 7th time the walls came tumbling down (Joshua 6). I knew God would complete his work pertaining to Olivier's healing in room 7.

I started negotiating with the speech therapist to allow Olivier to eat. She would be the one to determine the safety of feeding him real food and also whether the feeding tube should be discontinued.

The speech therapist inquired how I knew Olivier was hungry. Although at this point she believed Olivier was truly communicating with me, she was still unsure at which intellectual level.

Here I will pause to explain medically the implications of brain injuries. Brain injuries can be tricky in determining the true status of a patient. Neurologists avoid giving a positive prognosis due to their uncertainty of the patient's full recovery. They rely on many tests and what they see physically happening with the patient before they can even pronounce a full recovery. Much depends on the patient himself. Nobody can predict how well they will come out of a state of unconsciousness because it depends on where in the brain the injury has occurred and the severity of the injury, amongst other factors. A person may come out with a combination of physical, cognitive and psychological difficulties that need special attention. In this instance, Olivier was showing rapid improvement since Easter Sunday, in my opinion. The doctors thought differently and used what is referred to as a PTA (Post traumatic amnesia) score to check his level of consciousness daily.

Post traumatic amnesia (PTA) is a phase people go through following a significant brain injury, when they are confused, disoriented and have trouble with their memory. They may not be able to recall their date of birth, or may not know where they are or what has happened.

People in PTA will be tested on a daily basis with a test called the West Mead PTA scale. This test has 12 questions, some concerning orientation such as 'what day is it?', or 'what year is it?' Other questions assess memory such as remembering objects or faces. This test is repeated each day and a score of one point is given for every correct answer. A person is considered to be emerging from PTA when their scores increase but they have to score 12 out of 12 three times in a row to be considered out of PTA.

Sometimes it is possible for someone to be oriented but still get the memory component of the test wrong, which tells us that he or she is not able to lay down new memories. Although most people come out of PTA eventually there is no set time for this because each person is different and each head injury heals at a different rate. Some people are in PTA for a few days or weeks; others for much longer.

For Olivier, his PTA score was always low. His inability to communicate via oral language impacted greatly his prognosis.

I felt compelled to explain to the speech therapist the incident I related earlier about Olivier eating a full bowl of spaghetti on his own at 12 months of age. More than anything, it was intuitive on my part as his grandmother and caretaker. I knew he had not ingested solid food for over three weeks now he was actually feeling better and well enough to eat. He was only being fed through a nasogastric tube (NG tube). This is a narrow bore tube which is passed into the stomach via the nose. It is used for short- or medium term nutritional support, and also for aspiration of stomach contents. This NG tube had been inserted since his arrival in ICU.

The speech therapist explained Olivier would need to be able to stick out his tongue and swallow water before receiving soft foods. She would then listen to the regurgitation sound in his throat to ensure that he wouldn't choke.

Chapter 13

The Failed Test

On Tuesday, April 14, I sat at Olivier's bedside reading and praying for him as was my habit.

The speech therapist came along to Olivier's room with an assistant. Armed with drinks, glass, straws, and soft cookies that melt in one's mouth, all was in place to perform the test on Olivier. Her assistant first poured the drink into the glass then inserted the straw.

I was exuberant with the belief that my grandson would soon speak. After weeks of going through this ordeal, it was comforting to know we were soon to leave this hospital and Singapore back to KL. Lost in my thoughts, I jerked back to reality and concentrated on the test.

"Open your mouth and stick out your tongue, Olivier," was the command from the speech therapist. I looked at Olivier who stared into space seemingly ignoring her.

After a few more attempts she told me Olivier was suffering from aphasia.

Aphasia is a communication disorder that results from damage to the parts of the brain that contain language, typically in the left half of the brain. Individuals who experience damage to the right side of the brain may have additional difficulties beyond speech and language issues. Aphasia may cause difficulties in speaking, listening, reading, and writing, but does not affect intelligence. Individuals with aphasia may also have other problems, such as dysarthria, apraxia, or swallowing problems.

She planned to work with other speech-language pathologists (SLP) to find activities to improve specific language skills affected by damage to the brain. The SLP would also help Olivier develop and use strategies to improve overall communication in a variety of situations. Later on in recovery, the SLP would work with a vocational specialist to help Olivier return to school. A neurologist psychologist was also recommended.

Olivier with a therapist

My dream of going home was slowly being crushed by the realization that according to this report, there was a longer road to recovery! My faith refused to accept this report!

I needed to coax Olivier to do this simple exercise so he could pass the test! Somehow I knew that although it looked as if he was suffering from aphasia, he was not. Every word the Lord spoke to me pointed towards healing yet the medical teams report was the opposite! My spiritual belief had to surpass my medical knowledge in order to bring about Olivier's healing!

After the therapist left, I comforted a very frustrated Olivier. He flailed his legs around in defiance of this report. He understood everything that was said by the therapist. I told him if he wanted to prove them wrong, he needed to simply cooperate.

Convincing Olivier of the inevitable, lay in knowing this child's personality. This trait manifested in his gene inherited from his mother who got it from her father! You could not make Olivier do anything that he didn't want to do! The same went with Alesea and Clement! They all had stubborn streaks which ran deep in their DNA. I'm being rather sarcastic right now but during the time, it was not funny! This character defect had proven to be an asset in my husband's life and in Alesea's, but now Olivier's future depended on his explicit cooperation. I had to use reverse psychology.

I lowered my voice in such a way Olivier would not feel threatened or frustrated but rather confident that I was on his side. "Olivier dear, you want to eat, don't you?" I knew his response was yes, though he gave no indication by nodding his head. I went on in a sing-sing like voice, "in order to eat, you have to listen and obey the simple instructions given to you by the nice therapist." This got his attention. "Let me show you what she requires you to do."

Just then Rose walked into the room from her break. "Bring me water in a cup and a spoon please, Rose," I said without taking my attention from Olivier. She quickly put her things down and brought the utensils I requested then she went to stand on the opposite side of the bed to watch what I would do. "Now, stick out your tongue Olivier." Immediately, when I said it, he did it! I knew I had to remain calm and not get excited which might cause him to retract back into his shell. "Now, Rose, put a few drops of water on Olivier's tongue please." She did so. "Can you swallow that Olivier?" This time he nodded.

We did this exercise a few times again to insure there were no further effects of aphasia. Then with no additional mention of the incident, we finished the evening in our normal fashion. However, I took Rose aside and asked her to continue this exercise later on that evening and the next day. I would get the speech pathologist to return.

A few days later on Friday, April 17, again excitement coursed through my veins. I went on my faith walk, talking to God, praying and proclaiming victory over aphasia and any other issues that could keep Olivier from recovering fully. I returned from my walk for the visit by the team of doctors.

We had been given another doctor who was in charge of ward 7. He was Chinese and also a neurologist. His mannerisms were curt and professional. It was evident he commanded respect from his peers and other team members. He had been given Olivier's history which was evident by his bedside manner with him. His full attention was directed on Olivier who complied with his requests.

I asked the doctor if I would be able to see the speech therapist again that afternoon. He promised to arrange a visit for us according to her availability.

The day dragged on with no sign of the therapist. Olivier had been sipping water and sticking out his tongue regularly at this point. I was certain he had become such a natural that once the therapist did appear, it would be second nature for him to comply.

I had questioned the head nurse a few times but by 5 p.m. the therapist still hadn't shown up. I had been reluctant to leave Olivier's room not wanting to miss her visit. Finally, around 5:30 p.m. she came, extremely apologetic for her delay.

"Olivier's been sipping water with a straw," I said to her nonchalantly, "Can't he eat now?"

"Let me see", she said, bringing out her stethoscope in disbelief.

Rose and I had stuck close to the room most of the day, only venturing out for a few minutes at a time. We didn't want to run the risk of missing the therapist visit.

"Rose, please give Olivier sips of water," I said, not wanting Olivier to withdraw from the assistant whom the therapist brought with her. The therapist watched curiously as Olivier took small sips of water from a straw. She brought out the cookies from earlier and gave to him to eat. All the while, she kept the stethoscope to his throat listening to the regurgitation sounds.

"Well," the therapist concluded, "Olivier is able to swallow without any hindrances. I'll order a soft diet for him to have tomorrow morning. The kitchen has already closed. I'll have the dietician send a form for you to complete his menu. Good job Olivier." She still seemed stunned at this unexplainable turn of events. I sat smugly in the background silently thanking God.

With that she left to scribble notes in his file at the nurse's station.

Then I stood up and sighed. My heart sank. All of this long anticipation, only for Olivier to have to wait another several hours before eating. I saw the disappointment in his face and reassured him. Signaling to Rose to remain in the room, I slipped past the nursing station where the therapist was still busy writing on Olivier's chart.

As I was certain of our victory in this situation, I didn't want to wait any longer on God's promised miracle. Faith is NOW! Now that we had the green light to eat, I didn't want to wait another day. I knew that as Jesus commanded in Mark 5 to give the damsel something to eat, that this would be crucial for Olivier's healing. This was the final piece of the puzzle.

I hurried to the ground floor, the hospital layout being quite familiar to me now. Scanning the various shops I searched to see what Olivier could digest easily and most importantly, what would be appealing for him to taste after days of starvation!

I knew the soft diet ordered by the doctor would not be appealing enough to be eaten by Olivier. He is a very picky eater and despite his chunkiness, he wouldn't eat just anything.

My eyes fell upon a waffle shop which made hot waffles to order. Olivier loved waffles and adored Nutella. I thought to myself, waffles should be soft enough and if I can put a thin layer of Nutella on top of one then that should do the trick.

You must understand at this point I was not being governed by laws of 'common sense' or logic. I had gone way past that stage. I knew that the most nourishing food to give him would be liquid or a bland diet but I also knew Olivier wouldn't be motivated to eat that type of food.

My eyes were glued to the waffle shop so I went in without further thought, ordered two plain waffles with Nutella on the side. Gathering my loot disguised in a plain bag, I rushed out of the shop finding the quickest elevator to the 7th floor.

By now, faith had sunk its teeth deep. I was already past being victorious. I could see my grandson eating, talking and walking. I could just feel it! Arriving on the 7th floor, I sauntered past the nursing station, the speech therapist nowhere in sight. Entering the room I found Rose curled up in a comfortable chair near the window reading. Olivier was busy watching a program on television.

Not wanting to disturb Rose for this experiment, I went to the obscured side of the bed perhaps in the back of my mind realizing that she would question my intentions.

I carefully raised the head of Olivier's bed to sitting position. Placing the waffles on a plate on his bedside table Olivier began to salivate. I first spread a thin layer of Nutella on one waffle indicating to Olivier he could eat. I fed him one tiny piece giving him sips of water after each bite. I watched his esophagus closely to insure he swallowed the food properly. I tried to feed him slowly, but Olivier wolfed down the waffle hungrily! He finished one waffle fully expecting to eat the second. I watched as he ate the last morsel and asked if he had gotten it all down and whether he was finished "Did you get it down Olivier?" Fully expecting him to nod his head but instead he said, "It is done"!

What a glorious, victorious moment that was for me! Those words spoken by the Savior himself on a cross on Calvary sailed down 2000 plus years to the 7th floor room 7 at BEH Hospital were uttered by my grandson! When Jesus said it was done, the veil in the temple was torn into and we immediately had access into the

Holy of Holies. His finished work on the cross meant that our sins and sicknesses had been taken care of and it was done!

Fully aware of Olivier's personality, not wanting to alarm him or cause him to withdraw into his shell, I called Rose's name softly. "Rose, would you come here, please," I said gesturing calmly at the empty plate, "Olivier has finished his waffle." Rose immediately understood by my tone that she should also remain calm and collected. She too spoke softly to Olivier, "Olivier, you finished your food," she applauded his efforts, "good Olie," as we fondly had nicknamed him.

Olivier replied to Rose with speech. I then explained to Rose how to feed him as I searched for my cell phone to call his grandpa.

I knew that his grandpa would be on his way to Singapore most likely in heavy traffic but I couldn't contain my excitement any longer. I gave glory to God for His Mighty work and was anxious to share this miraculous occurrence with Clement.

Getting Clement on the phone I spoke to him in French so that Olivier wouldn't understand me. Hearing my words, he pulled over to the shoulder of the road clearly shaken. Initially, he thought I was joking. In 'talking' he assumed I meant our usual means of communication with Olivier.

On a previous occasion Clement had asked that I place Olivier on the phone. That was the first and only time that Olivier had struggled to speak. In fact, he had become so frustrated not being able to make intelligent speech, he never attempted again. At that time his voice was merely grunts and he had remained silent till now. I knew he was plagued with a spirit of aphasia but God delivered him!

Although I knew that the Lord had said he would speak after eating food, I was still so amazed such fluent language had come out of Olivier's mouth tonight and was visibly shaken by his outburst. It was as if his tongue had been loosed supernaturally! I knew that another miracle had just taken place!

Olivier and his grandpa are extremely close. If anyone could get him to speak more, it would be his grandpa.

"Grandpa is on the phone Olivier. He's coming from KL today to see you," I exclaimed, "What would you like him to bring you?"

"Hawaiian pizza", Olivier said, obviously having forgotten his attempt to speak a week ago.

"Tell Grandpa yourself," I said putting the phone to his ear. "Olivier's on the phone," I said to Clement, shouting in the mouthpiece in the background.

"Hi Olivier," Clement said nervously, not wanting Olivier to retreat.

"Hey Grandpa".

"What do you want me to bring you from KL?"

"Hawaiian Pizza," Olivier retorted.

We knew our little boy was back because this was his favorite food in the world. We found out later from Olivier's parents that this was his number one pizza to eat in the USA. He had also eaten it with his grandpa numerous times.

By all indications, Olivier seemed to have his priorities in place. His mind was intact just as the Lord had said and indeed he was well!

We give our God, glory, honor and majesty for his mighty works!

Chapter 14

<u>Recovery</u>

The road to complete recovery beckoned to us. That night Clement had brought the promised pizza but way too late for Olivier to consume all of it. He only had a slice and the rest was kept for breakfast.

April 18, Saturday morning, Clement recorded on his cell phone, Olivier eating pizza. Obviously, I had to come clean to the staff doctor and admit my "waffle crime". He was equally thrilled Olivier was eating and quite surprised he was also talking. Of course his explanation was related to science and psychology, but I knew it had been God.

The full neurological team didn't work during the weekend therefore we were only able to inform Olivier's new doctor. However; later on in the morning, one of the neurologist who was from the Middle East and had been following Olivier since his first day of arrival came into his room. We'll refer to her as Dr. Nabul.

Dr. Nabul had captured a snippet of Olivier's personality while working with him and had been particularly aggressive in getting him better.

When she saw Olivier sitting up and learned he was eating and talking, she sought to explain by using a medical explanation as well, although she seemed happy enough to listen to my story of what had actually occurred with him. She checked his PTA score which had now gone up significantly compared to Easter Sunday.

Clement kept track of the time difference between Singapore and the USA, so that we could call Carmelo and Alesea to inform them of this wonderful miraculous occurrence in their son.

We had Olivier up out of bed propped up on pillows on the sofa. He had been eating nonstop since the previous night. It was as if he wanted to make up for lost time! The small fridge in the room was bursting to the seams with drinks he requested as well as drinks the dietician brought on the trays.

"Let's Skype Mom and Dad," Grandpa said to Olivier once the time was right.

"Ok," Olivier responded.

It is worthy to note that from the evening before till that morning Olivier was speaking to us and even to the doctors in his normal fashion. We didn't want to bombard him with questions to ascertain how much he remembered but the questions we asked regarding time, place and people he had responded to appropriately.

Olivier remembered getting sick in KL and being hospitalized at Gleneagles. He also recalled who his friends were, the name of his school and home room teacher. He was eager to get back to KL and return to school but he didn't want to speak to his best friend yet.

When Olivier first arrived in September, he had convinced Grandpa he needed a phone in KL. All his school mates had phones and what if something happened that required him getting in touch with us? His argument had been persuasive enough for Grandpa to give him his iPhone. This iPhone had become Olivier's regular companion and while he seldom used it to call or message us; he was always playing one video game or another! I had to constantly remind him to put his phone down! We were therefore quite surprised that he was not interested in his phone anymore. Also we realized he had forgotten his password. This was all a normal occurrence due to the trauma he had suffered.

We used Grandpa's phone to contact his parents. They also knew to display a normal reaction of relative calm as not to scare the boy. However, they couldn't help but be overjoyed while speaking to Olivier.

"Hey Olivier, how are you doing?" his mom said eyes glossing filling up with tears that threatened to flow any moment.

"I'm good," Olivier said with his usual response that he still uses today.

"I'm glad you're doing better son," Carmelo chimed in.

All of a sudden, we noticed Olivier switched his tone of voice. He started behaving like he was three or four! When his dad asked what he was watching on television, he told him Elmo because he only wanted to watch happy stories.

We knew this was part of the internal turmoil Olivier was unable to express by having his parents so far away. This void had not been seen while he was well, but apparently the sickness had triggered it.

The fact that Olivier had been speaking to Grandpa, Rose, the doctors and myself in a normal way encouraged us all. We knew this would be only a momentary thing.

After a while, the Skype phone call ended, but Olivier kept the television on children's programs and also began to respond to us like he had spoken to his parents. Both Clement and I looked at one another. I raised an eyebrow to Rose, but we all knew not to comment on this new development while in Olivier's presence.

As I mentioned earlier in the introduction, one thing we praised Olivier for was his command of speech. When he first learned to talk, he didn't speak a lot of gibberish. It was as if he went from "mama" "papa" to Mom and Dad. He also began to speak like his parents and their college generation.

Although we were not fully present during all those years due to our travels, most people who met Olivier noted how proficient in speech he was. My brother Tommie who doesn't talk much himself related the following story to me.

They were once at a family gathering where Olivier and his parents were present. Olivier wasn't really talking or interacting with anyone. After a long while, my brother who was in his fifties asked Olivier a question, "How you doing buddy? You're not gonna talk to anyone today?" To my brother's surprise, Olivier started speaking to him! But not a conversation you would expect a 4 year old to have! He talked to him about going fishing, basically he told my brother about all the fishing trips he'd been on, bait he'd used and fish he'd caught. Needless to say, my brother was surprised that a four year old would speak in this manner. So much so, he related this story to me when I came home that summer.

I hope you get the picture I'm trying to paint. Olivier didn't go through the usual channels of making conversation that a boy his age would experience. He seemed to be a little man in a child's body!

My theory was perhaps the inability or lack of having related in childlike language when he was small, caused Olivier to do so now after the trauma. No doubt he was terrified on the inside due to what had happened to him, using this as a coping mechanism to survive. I decided to leave him in that space for a while fully aware that God had promised complete recovery before his mom arrived.

Another challenge was getting Olivier out of bed to walk. Clement used a game to get Olivier to attempt walking.

"You have to dominate your limbs Olivier, your body needs to say, body get up and legs move. Body speaks to legs and legs obey." Clement told him.

Clement put Olivier's right foot on his left foot and did the same with right. He basically used his sheer energy to lift Olivier holding him up as he gained strength to walk.

Olivier got up laughing with Clement. They 'walked' together until we were told he could use the wheelchair. I knew this would deter him, nevertheless I gave in. The physiotherapist and occupational therapist would have their work cut out for them on Monday!

Clement repeated his 'body and soul' sessions most of the day until Olivier was able to walk a few steps without assistance. More praises to our God!

Lastly, my prayer had been to present Olivier to his mom whole. God promised me He would. I had read 2 Kings 4:8 and 1 Kings 17:22 after one of my faith walks. Both stories are about two women whose sons had died and prophets had resurrected them to life. In both instances the sons had been presented to their mothers healthy and whole. This was the Word of God I now held fast to.

Chapter 15

Paradigm Shift

From Monday, April 20 to Friday, April 24, the day my daughter was to arrive, Olivier was busy with a flurry of activities. His daily visits with the physiotherapist and occupational therapist helped his movements become more fluid and this totally rehabilitated him. Olivier was walking more and more without his wheelchair and also performaing strengthening exercises to help him to relearn how to grasps objects, shower, tie his shoes and button his clothes. Every day we saw more progress in him.

Tuesday, April 21, I decided to talk to Olivier about his language. The room was quiet; Clement had returned to KL on Sunday, just Rose and I stayed in Olivier's room.

Olivier would only sleep at night if he knew I was at the hospital. So I had started to stay nights at the hospital and showered during the day at my friend's. I would sometimes take a nap after my shower if time permitted.

Olivier and I were alone in the room. Perhaps Rose had stepped out for lunch, I can't remember exactly. I felt like it was time for me to have a heart to heart talk with Olivier about what had happened. I explained to him in detail the essence of his illness in which we had spoken of before and he knew from previous discussion much of what I was saying.

My monologue brought us to the present day, physical and mental preparation to enable that he return to ISKL and eventually to the USA with his mom.

"Your mom arrives on Friday with Sanaa, you're aware of that right?"

"Yes," Olivier responded in a soft, meek voice.

"You'll be returning to your 4th grade classroom, isn't that correct?"

"Yes," he repeated this affirmation.

"Wouldn't you like to return to your friends, play games and go on outings?"

"Yes," he said.

"How do you plan to relate to your friends, on this level or the previous level?"

"Like before," Olivier responded.

"Well don't you want to talk like you used to?"

"Sure, what do I need to do?" he asked.

"You've been through a traumatic experience Olivier that most people will never go through. But now you must give yourself permission to move forward."

"How do I do that?" he inquired in a flat tone, his eyes glued to the usual Disney Channel he had been watching as of late.

I walked over and handed him the remote control, "You need to change what you're watching. Go back to your National Geographic Channels and the various channels you watched prior to your illness. I even give you permission to use my phone to play your old games if you like."

I was really overstepping my set boundaries for him, but I truly wanted normalcy in his life. I knew that Olivier was capable of speaking normal because he had done that the first day he started to speak. This was more of a mental issue than a brain latency one.

Taking the remote from my hand, Olivier pointed it towards the television and found a better child educational program like he used to watch. Immediately he spoke in a normal fashion to me and has done so ever since! He had a paradigm shift, an epiphany moment, if you will!

I encouraged Olivier to communicate with his friends on 'Hangouts' using my phone. He had told them on a group chat that he thought he was four years old again. He had started sharing honestly with his peers what he had been going through. All of them had been worried about him and were anxious for him to recover and return to school. They encouraged him greatly and did not make fun of him. They, too, wanted him well.

Chapter 16

Alesea and Sanaa's Arrival in Singapore

Finally, the day dawned when Alesea and Sanaa were to arrive in Singapore. Clement took off work early in order to drive them.

Olivier was walking almost completely without use of his wheelchair. He was able to shower and dress and feed himself. He was just about his old self again.

Alesea had been invited by the doctors at BEH to have a consultation explaining Olivier's post condition and the way forward. They also asked a psychologist, who specializes in neurology, to be present and to interview Olivier. This meeting was to be scheduled on a day that suited Alesea as she had to fly all the way from the USA.

I anticipated that the various reports from the doctors would not give God all the glory and honor He deserved. I was not prepared for God to be excluded, so I prayed that God's Word and God's report would prevail.

Several times in advance, I had informed the doctors of Alesea's arrival as otherwise we could have actually left for KL a week earlier. We only remained in Singapore so that the doctors could speak to Alesea on a personal basis and let her know what to expect concerning her son's prognosis.

On arrival in Singapore that Friday afternoon, April 24, Alesea went straight to the hospital, exhausted from her long flight. We were all overwhelmed to see her and Sanaa. Olivier was especially happy to see his mom and sister. They had a great reunion together.

That morning, the staff doctor repeatedly had asked me of Alesea's estimated time of arrival. Then suddenly the strangest thing happened; he burst into the room declaring that he had an emergency and had to leave immediately. I was greatly puzzled. Olivier's regular neurologist, whom had seen him from the first day in the emergency room, also had a family emergency and could not make the appointment! I was now a little more than irate. We had remained in Singapore for this appointment. Alesea had flown 22 hours with a toddler then driven five hours in a car and everyone cancelled! In the end, only the chief neurologist was able to come and deliver the report.

The buildup that the medical team had made to do a presentation on Alesea's behalf speaking to her about Olivier's diagnosis, recovery and way forward had been mind boggling. Clement and I were the legal guardians however, the team had insisted on meeting Alesea.

We waited for some time for Olivier's other doctor to commence the promised meeting, but after a while we were informed that this doctor had taken leave for that day. The meeting the medical team had so carefully planned had disintegrated into thin air!

Instead, the head of neurology, who happens to be a very nice man, came to give a factual report which agreed with that of the Lord's to a certain extent! It was plausible and gave a promising way forward. He left us with a letter, however, which requested that educational institutions should not test Olivier due to his diminished cognitive state.

God remains Sovereign in all that He does. That day, He received all the glory and honor for Olivier's recovery. There was NO man standing to say, we used medical science for his recovery; none. Even in the reports, there was NOTHING specific besides the diagnosis of Mycoplasma that the doctors could underline. Sure they had used antibiotics to fight MP but other than that, everything surrounding the days Olivier was 'asleep' till the day he woke up defied human knowledge.

In the aftermath, I understood clearly that God did not want any human being to be given the glory for His mighty acts. While the doctors were busy explaining away Olivier's recovery with human nuances, God was saying, I am that I Am! I AM the Great Physician. Give Me the Glory! That was the only explanation that I could think of!

Chapter 17

Return to Kuala Lumpur

Olivier returned to KL to complete his fourth grade school year. He also had a few physical therapy sessions recommended by his doctor. Of course I didn't feel these sessions were necessary and neither did the therapist! But I didn't want it to appear as if I was non-compliant. Olivier's mom was now present and was involved in his healthcare.

At the onset of Olivier's visit to the physical therapist, she questioned his reason for being there even though she had the report in front of her. He looked perfectly fine and mastered most of the work given to him. I showed pictures of his condition only a week or two earlier, only then did she understand and comply with the instructions provided by the physical therapist from Singapore.

I felt the work presented to Olivier was really a waste of time. Olivier was fully mobile at this point and dreaded going. The physical therapist also didn't challenge him. One day, I was surprised to see my old physical therapist working at Gleneagles. I asked if he would take Olivier's case. I knew him to be tough and knew he would make Olivier's sessions worthwhile. I wasn't mistaken about that. He concluded that Olivier was meeting all the expectations given him on the list. Olivier would require just two more days of therapy and during these days, the therapist provided challenges that Olivier could not even meet before his illness. That's just how well Olivier had improved.

Olivier returned to a very excited fourth grade class. On his first day back, both Alesea and I were with him. Olivier insisted on not having any special treatment or recognition. He simply wanted to walk to his desk and sit down. It turns out there was a special presentation that day so he could easily mix with the other students in the common area. Then he went with his classmates back to his home room.

The nurse who was my colleague, the school manager, and bus assistant were all informed of Olivier's request for no special attention. For us this was simply a precautionary measure and in line with the doctor's orders.

The recommendation from the doctor was; only half days for Olivier, however when I went to collect him, he wanted to stay with his classmates for lunch. I reminded Olivier that he should rest in the afternoons so he could recuperate more quickly. For Olivier, this was bit ridiculous since he knew he was well.

The next day Olivier again asked me to pick him up after lunch and by Wednesday he was up to doing full days including catching the bus home! We preferred a much happier Olivier at school with his classmates than a grumpy one at home complaining.

He showed no signs of fatigue and didn't seem to require more rest than usual. Nights tended to be long for him as he didn't like sleeping by himself. The first night, he requested I sleep in his bedroom like we had done at BEH. He felt an extra measure of security with me there and was able to enjoy sound sleep.

The second night, I prayed with Olivier like I had the first night, but did not sleep in his room. I instructed him to pray to the Lord when he was afraid. If he needed his mom or me, we were both within earshot. We also left a lamp on in the hall as we had always done in the past for him. But this time he wanted his door open.

Olivier's best reunion was that with Bailey our old dog who we got the chance to visit. He also got to introduce her to Sanaa, who loved Bailey instantly. Although Bailey had bonded with her new family and had been spoiled with a lap pool as well as a personal bedroom, she had not forgotten Olivier. They had been fast friends from the beginning of their acquaintance. Olivier often commented, "Bailey looks like she's smiling." And indeed I believe this time she was.

Chapter 18

Completing Fourth Grade

The end of the school year had been the proper time established for Olivier to return to his parents. With one exception, I was supposed to have taken him home over the summer.

Now Alesea and Sanaa would return with Olivier once school was done.

It was actually good for Alesea to attend the end of the year events including Olivier's last appointment with his teacher. His teacher told Alesea that she was surprised at the outstanding progress Olivier had made in spite of his weeks of absentees. She concluded how he was producing better work than before! In fact, I felt he had returned to us much better than before in all regards!

It was as if he had a new lease on life enjoying things he had previously taken advantage of. For instance he loved going swimming and playing in the park. These are activities we had to beg him to do in the past!

We also noticed he had less interest in his phone. He also did not want to abuse the use of his X-box.

We have all been amazed and astonished at God's miracle working power in Olivier's life. We are forever grateful!

This is God! Let Faith Arise!

Chapter 19

<u>Olivier's Birthday Party</u>

When school ended, we threw Olivier an early 10th birthday party with the classmates he had selected. In our apartment building, downstairs we had a pool as well as facilities available where we held the event. The way Olivier jumped ran and splashed in the pool, no one would ever have guessed this thriving healthy boy had endured the horrible ordeal he had been through only a few weeks prior. We did not restrain Olivier from doing anything he wanted to do at that party! He deserved to live and live life in abundance! His friends thoroughly enjoyed his party as if their friendship had never been interrupted.

The birthday cake with 10 candles lit held a very solemn and symbolic meaning for me. The children raised their voices to sing Happy Birthday but my mind was far away. How gracious of our Lord to grant us His peace by *Releasing the Dove* of healing over Olivier's life---the extended olive branch.

We often tease Olivier saying welcome to double digits. But in all fairness, ten is a wonderful number to behold. My Pastor Moss loves dissecting numbers in scripture and has sort of converted me to doing the same.

In the Bible there are several numbers that have certain biblical significations. Ten is made up of the number 4 which according to the Bible is the number of physical creation while the number 6 is the number of man. As such it signifies testimony, law and completeness of order. In Geneses 1 we see the phrase '**God said**' 10 times which is indicative of his creative power. I believe God said, "Let Olivier live," and he did.

There were Ten Commandments given to man to follow as a reflection of His expectations of mankind. The first 4 are vertical towards God and the last six are horizontal (human relationships which I've touched on before.) The fact is, the 10 commandments if kept, would be all that society would require to live in peace and harmony with both God and man. This is truly the peace that only the dove of the Holy Spirit brings.

But the most interesting fact of all to me about the number 10 is this: ten generations of man lived on the earth before the flood waters came and swept away all those who were disobedient. Noah, from the tenth generation was 600 years old when he and seven other family members entered the ark.

I have spoken before regarding the signification of the number 7. Olivier's last room number being 7 was no coincidence but was all ordained in the perfect plan of God. 7 is also the number of completion and the number of victory.

Most importantly, I believe the story of Noah and my personal legacy is definitely intertwined. The fact that God put his rainbow in the sky as a reminder to Noah of his covenant of peace and the same at my wedding as a sign of his covenant of peace is paramount. The dove that Noah sent out returned with an Olive branch signifying life was upon the earth was the verse of scripture that I took to name Olivier.

Olivier once told me he wanted to change his name to Noah I believe, because the name Olivier was too difficult for people to pronounce! I now think with a chuckle, "I wonder if his story would have been any different if we had?"

I am brought back to the present time, picturing the scene of Olivier's 10th birthday party again, the swimming pool venue resembling an ark, the swimming pool representing the deluge and the children….well just children, the only animals being the stuffed plastic inflatable ones scattered around the outskirts of the pool. In my mind's eye, I can't help but gaze upwards toward the expanse of sky hoping to get a glimpse of a rainbow….and a dove.

Postlude

July 29, 2015

Olivier has now been back home in the USA for over a month. Just this week, I received exceptional news from my daughter, she had attempted to book a follow up appointment with a neurologist in the USA. Her general practitioner (GP) denied her request because he did not find any symptoms that warranted a visit to a neurologist. Alesea was quite upset about this. I reassured her by giving her the rhema word God had planted in my heart supernaturally. When she asked me why, I reminded her of God's Word. She was thinking in terms of having a neurologist in place, just in case this situation happened again. I assured her that it would not! I reminded her of what God had spoken when we were still at BEH in Singapore. I explained to her about Faith.

Faith is taking God at His Word. 'I know that God is going to do this for me one day' isn't faith. You're not in agreement with God. Faith is NOW! He sent His Word and healed them and delivered them from their destructions. (Psalms 107:20 NIV).

God was just speaking to me through His Word during Olivier's convalescence. Listen, what you do in the secret place, in the quiet, when things are going fine, sets you up to access the Blesser when things are not going fine!

The Word of God became more real to me than the doctors or the person sitting next to me. The Bible reads in John 1:1,

"In the beginning was the Word and the Word was with God and the Word was God."

1 John 1 states,

"That which was from the beginning, which we have heard, which we have seen with our eyes, which we have looked at and our hands have touched this we proclaim concerning the Word of life."

We, New Testament Christians, have not seen Christ with our physical eyes, but we can see Him with our spiritual eyes through His Word.

I read the Word of God very differently now. It reverberates in my very bones. I now know what Jeremiah meant in 20:9:

"But if I say, 'I will not mention his word or speak anymore in his name' his word is in my heart like a fire, a fire shut up in my bones. I am weary of holding it in."

Relating this experience to my daughter was like recharging my faith batteries! I knew that God could not go back on His Word. Whether Alesea found a neurologist to do a follow up visit or not was of no consequence for Olivier. He is well!

Alesea phoned again this week from the USA to let me know that Olivier had been accepted in a most prestigious private school in her area. This was excellent news. Although his doctor in Singapore had requested that he should not be tested at any educational institution in his first six months being back due to his diminished cognitive state, the school either ignored the doctor's request or did not acknowledge his recommendations, because Olivier was given an extensive entrance test and he aced it! This is a child whom the doctors said would require at least six months before he could be academically tested due to the nature of his recent illness.

Even in the USA, God has continued to work miracle after miracle in the life of this little boy and I want to give God the glory!

Talitha Coumi - Let Faith Arise!

The woman with the issue of blood in Mark 5 was probably a wealthy woman and had spent all her money going from one doctor to the other and for 12 years her case remained the same. But one day she said in her heart, I shall be made whole.

Faith brings about determination, you must have a stubborn spirit! She had access to the Blesser! Despite her condition and knowing that she was not allowed to mix with people, she determined to touch the Blesser! Many people were touching Jesus and healing virtue didn't leave his body, why was it that when she touched Him it did? Her faith ignited her healing! Faith is taking God at His Word! She had already determined in her heart that she would be healed once she could access Jesus! There was a manifestation of the miraculous because her faith was backed with the anointing!

To get a better understanding of faith, read this analogy: When I lived in Congo sometimes we didn't have electricity therefore needed a generator. Once the generator is switched on there's always electricity, but there will be no power supply in the house, no lights, until you connect the plug to a socket that's connected to the generator and switch it on! Only then will you know the generator is producing power! The power has to be switched on for a manifestation for it to give you light. So is faith in the spiritual realm. The power is already available in Jesus who is the same yesterday, today and forever. Whether you need healing, financial blessing, or marital restoration, the formula is the same. You must switch on your faith and connect to the Blesser who is none other than Jesus Christ!

Mark 11:24 (NIV):

"Therefore, I say unto you. What things so ever ye desire when ye pray, believe that ye receive them and ye shall have them."

Three remarkable words, believe, receive and have. If there is anything that you desire in the will of God, believe first, before you can have it.

Olivier had the best neurologists in all of Asia, yet God is the Great Physician. I took Him at His Word, told the doctors to remove the breathing tube, and to take him off the medications that were sedating him, because he was breathing and alive! Of course they thought I was foolish and crazy, but my husband supported me and believed God. On Easter Day, He did not leave Olivier's bedside. He would not leave Singapore for KL until he saw a sign of life!

Clement had faith to believe that HE WOULD SEE A SIGN before leaving AND HE DID!

The doctors collaborated and at my word removed the tube and Olivier was breathing on his own just as God said!

- The woman in Mark 5 with the issue of blood touched Jesus and her faith made her whole
- I believed God's Word and had Olivier taken off of certain medication including life support in ICU and my faith made him whole.
- Draw your faith from God's Word and then declare it with your mouth; because faith is not released until it is declared.

Remember Thomas' kind of faith in John 20:25. Thomas was Jesus disciple who would NOT believe that Jesus was alive until he thrust his hand in His side.

He said, "Until I see, I will not believe."

There is yet another kind of Faith which is Abraham's kind of faith. You can find this in Romans: 4:17-21 :

"As it is written, I have made thee a father of many nations, before him whom he believes, even God who quickeneth the dead, and calleth those things which be not as though they were. Who against hope believe in hope, that he might become the father of many nations, according to that which was spoken, so shall thy seed be. And being not weak in faith he considered not his own body now dead when he was about an hundred years old, neither yet the deadness of Sarah's womb. He staggered not as the promise of God though unbelief but was strong in faith, giving glory to God; and being full persuaded that what he had promised he was able to perform."

Important Insights Summarized from Olivier's Healing

1- You must believe and not doubt.

I had to get my husband Clement and Rose to have faith and believe.

"When Jesus went to Nazareth he could not do many miracles there because of their unbelief. A prophet is not known in his own country. Is this not Jesus the carpenter's son?" Mark 6:5 (NIV)

2- You must have faith.

"And without faith it is impossible to please God, because anyone who comes to him must believe that he exists and that he rewards those who earnestly seek him." Hebrews 11:5 (NIV)

3- A mustard seed is not very big. But this is the type of faith that God requires.

"Then came the disciples to Jesus apart, and said, why could not we cast him out? And Jesus said unto them, Because of your unbelief: for verily I say unto you, If ye have faith as a grain of mustard seed, ye shall say unto this mountain, Remove hence to yonder place; and it shall remove; and nothing shall be impossible unto you. Howbeit this kind goeth not out but by prayer and fasting".

4- Jesus is willing. I would not entertain any word from anyone who did not agree with God's word--neither my friends nor the doctors, nor my family.

In Matthew chapter 8 a man with leprosy came down and knelt at Jesus feet and said:

"'Lord if you are willing, you can make me clean'. Jesus reached out his hand and touched the man, 'I am willing (be healed,) be made clean' Jesus touched the untouchable!"

Matthew 8:8

"The centurion had a paralyzed servant at home and told Jesus, I am not worthy that you come under my roof, just speak the word and my servant will be healed."

The word became my bread and water. You cannot separate God from His word.

John 1:1 *"In the beginning was the Word and the Word was with God and the Word was God."*

I had gone on a fast before Easter and had said to the ladies from the Oasis Bible Study how I wanted to go on a Word fast. Be careful what you desire.

At one point, I was so desperate, I wanted to trade places with my grandson. God's word became so real to me. As I spoke to God, He spoke back to me through His Word.

John 15:17 (NIV)

"If you remain in me and my Words remain in you, you can ask whatever you wish, it will be done for you."

The Word- the promise

The second night in Singapore, Olivier's nanny arrived so I went to sleep at my friend's house. She and her husband's generosity was second to none. The Lord woke me up at 5:34 that morning. While I was waiting for her husband to drop me, I was talking to the Lord and he took me back to the digital read out on the clock.

Mark 5:34 (NIV)

"Daughter your faith has healed you, Go in peace and be freed from your suffering"

I knew that God was asking me to have faith for Olivier's healing and remain in peace. Fear is the absence of faith. Doubt is the absence of faith.

It was no coincidence that the Lord gave me the theme for the Women's Conference last year "Talitha Coumi, Arise" in Greek means, 'Little Girl, stand up!'

Read Mark 5:34-43. All of Olivier's healing hinged on these scriptures. When I arrived at the hospital, Olivier's condition had grown worse. Throughout the entire ordeal, Olivier had been lucid and talking. But that morning, when I spoke to him, Olivier acknowledged me but would not open his eyes. The doctors could not rouse him so they sent him immediately to ICU and put all the paraphernalia on and in him; breathing tube, heart monitor, 24 hour surveillance. It was God's grace that gave me that word that morning before arriving at the hospital.

My Pastor in KL often says one week away from church makes you weak! The scripture reads:

"If thou faint in the day of adversary, your strength is small." Proverbs 24:10.

"For we do not want you to be ignorant, brothers (and sisters) of the affliction we experienced in Asia. For we were so utterly burdened beyond our strength that we despaired of life itself" 2 Corinthians 1:8, 9.

This trial was designed to make us rely not on ourselves but on God who raises the dead.

To Him be all Glory and Honor Forever and Ever! Amen!

<u>Note:</u> Right at the time, I received the last draft from my editor; I was planning a surprise birthday lunch for my daughter Alesea. She informed me, my granddaughter was down with Mycoplasma Pneumonia. This marked nearly one year since Olivier's healing. I remembered the Word the Spirit had spoken to me in Nahum 1:9, 'Affliction shall not arise a second time.' I decreed supernatural healing over her and hastened to complete this book. I realized just how important this message could be in giving hope to those whose loved ones are suffering.

Praise Report

Photo of Olivier and his sister May 2016

Dear friends and family,

A year ago Olivier was recovering from a frightening health scare. His doctors although excellent, were concerned that he would not be able to recover fully physically, perform academically as he had in the past or excel in extracurricular activities.

But, your faith shown through your many prayers and well wishes have proved how powerful our God is. Please see an email from Olivier's school below. Not only did Olie make a FULL recovery, he excelled in everything he attempted including participating in honor's choir, soccer, guitar and being an honor roll student.

Isn't God good?!!! I hope this testimony has encouraged you as much as it has me. I'm so thankful for the wonderful support system I have in you and know that last year without you would have been unbearable. Thank you.

Love,

Alesea

Letter from the School

Parents,
This email is to inform you that your child will be recognized Monday, May 23, 2016 for qualifying for the A or A/B honor roll. Feel free to join us for Chapel Monday at 8:00 am.

Final Reflections

Dear Rhonda,

I finally finished reading Olivier's story. There is such a powerful message here for us all if we truly want to serve God. It is all about totally surrendering to His will as He did when he came in the flesh. Jesus surrendered to the will of the Father. He said I do nothing of my will but it is what I see my Father doing that I do. It was just wonderful and soul searching to see you in Singapore just following our Lord Jesus and doing what He was doing..... Wow!

These are my thoughts. I pray the Lord would help give understanding and correct where I am wrong.

Every aspect of Olivier's life, his name, his birth and the various incidents has a message from God. The illness and recovery story is an important story to share. I am so reluctant to call the incidence a story. I feel the word 'story' belittles the gravity of the message it communicates, which is, "Those who live in the Spirit must also strive to walk always in the Spirit, for it is only by walking in the Spirit we find peace that surpasses all understanding and solutions that bring rest when trials come or indeed when we are tested.

"His ways are not our ways. As the heaven is so far from the earth so are his ways so far from ours." Isaiah 55:8-9. We cannot remain where we are and walk with him in Spirit, we must always strive to make the necessary adjustments to enter into His will. Kuala lumper was life in the letter; Singapore for me represented life in the Spirit.

Olivier's name says it all. The name carries a message from Spirit of the Lord (The Dove). The Dove will always bring a message of peace, deliverance, liberty and spiritual rest in the lives of those that believe but one must tap into it to receive. It was wonderful to see you tap into it in Singapore. If you recall, when Noah sent the dove out, the dove always had a message and eventually came back with an olive leaf which communicated to Noah. Embedded in Olivier's life is a clear message to you and the household of the Lord to walk in the spirit always, only then would we receive from the Lord. We often are in the Spirit but do not always walk in the Spirit.

It was wonderful to see that once you were in Singapore in the Spirit and walking in the Spirit, the Word came forth and the food of the Spirit was what it was, water and waffles. Oliver's healing was in the Word and not in the letter, the letter representing the drugs. With the power in the Word, water and waffles did the trick. The Lord's ways are not ours.

The raven in contrast brought nothing back to Noah; it just kept going back and forth. The message was not with the Raven (the letter). The message is never in the letter. When we are operating in the letter we never tap into the message that brings God's solution, we simply go back and forth achieving nothing as I think happened in Kuala Lumpur.

The message is always with the Holy Spirit, the Dove, for THOSE THAT LIVE IN THE SPIRIT... Noah walked in the Spirit and the Dove communicated with Noah through the olive leaf.

Oliver's birth and the time spent with you also carry a powerful message. God chose for him to be born when and how he was born and like Samuel who had to live with Eli, it was also God's plan to have Olivier live with you for the time he did, to be nurtured by his spirit filled Grandma and not by his parents for God's purpose to be fulfilled. Had he not been with you the true meaning of his illness and recovery would have been lost. God had intended this incident to happen when Olivier was with you for God's purpose to be fulfilled. The message of this incident will bring revival to the hearts of many in Jesus name.

I remember the passage in the Bible about a deaf person in John 9:2 that the Lord had healed. His disciples had asked who had sinned for he had been deaf since birth and the Lord said none had sinned but it was so for the scriptures to be fulfilled. Also Jesus Christ our Lord was to be betrayed by Judas for the scriptures to be fulfilled and the confirmation came when it was done.

Jesus said it is finished!!! And He rose on the third day to sit at the right hand of God with all power on earth and in heaven given to him........The same confirmation came after Olivier had the food of the spirit. Healing began and total recovery followed! I am sure revival followed for many around him - this is power unto salvation. The Bible says that these are the signs that must follow those of us that believe, there must be healing, casting out of demons and nothing we eat affecting us.

Olivier needed to be at the right place with you for the message of his illness and healing to have meaning and indeed it has meaning. I believe his illness was not to lead to death but awaken or reawaken the dead in spirit, to ginger those of us who live in the spirit to also walk in the spirit and not in the flesh or the letter. The letter killeth but the Spirit brings to life (2 Corinthians 3:6).

The most prolific prophets sometimes walk in the flesh. If you recall, Samuel walked into Jesse's house in flesh worried about Saul finding out that he had gone to anoint the next King. With that mindset his choices were initially wrong until the Lord gingered him saying 'Samuel you look at the flesh, I look at the heart, Samuel was a little out of God's presence, and he needed to come back to his presence..... Samuel's thoughts had wondered off. The character of Samuel depicts Samuel as the messenger/prophet and also the message/word. In this instance, you are the messenger / prophet and Olivier is the word/ the message (the olive leaf).....the message has meaning and carries revival but only when interpreted by a messenger. (The messenger walked in the Spirit in Singapore.)

Walking in the letter killeth, in hindsight that was the clear message coming across, the overdose of the drugs from the various doctors of letters was killing him and waring with his spirit that required spiritual food from the messenger of God. All he needed was the Word, all the situation needed was the Word, the food of the Spirit which you tapped into as you proceeded from Kuala Lumper to Singapore.

The path to recovery was so different. The flesh as usual had failed and the Holy Spirit was now fully in control. Preparation was so different. Trust was totally on the only dependable God. Everybody was praying, different prayer groups who probably needed revival in their prayer lives had now joined in to witness the miracle of God...... The illness was then truly having meaning.

My dear Rhonda, it was interesting to see you in the full Spiritual gear, two significant adjustments I observed as you proceeded to Singapore.

The first adjustment maybe not planned but keyed into the flow - You travelled alone with Olivier and the accompanying Doctor, the powerful prayer moments during the journey must have been awesome. There was separation from flesh.
The second adjustment was the absolute faith in the word of God and actions that followed your belief? The greater in you had taken over.
I loved this part of the story that Jesus says in John 4:34 'My food is to do the will of Him that sent me." As you fed him with water and waffles, according to the will of God, it was done, healing had come. When Christ said the same words after being obediently nailed to the cross, there came spiritual healing for all that believe and freedom of access to walk in the Spirit and in the presence of God.

You know in all this I see the Elijah anointing upon you which is a powerful anointing to do great things in the name of our glorified Christ. Like Katherine Khulman, your healing ministry will explode when you fully dedicate your life to walking in the Spirit and letting the Lord do what only the Lord can do. You are there by the grace of God; your consciousness only needs to be aware of this.

As we have seen, God's ways are not our ways. He uses the simple things to confound the wise. Olivier was healed with water and waffles. Those hard sounding drugs you mentioned did not do the trick only put him in bondage. David if you recall brought down Goliath with a stone, all the weapons Saul gave him weighed him down, just as the drugs you gave Olivier weighed him down until you freed him by asking the doctors to stop and remove the tubes. Remember also Joshua, and the wall of Jericho, Moses and the Red Sea and Elijah and the prophets of Baal. The examples in the Bible abound............... God is truly awesome.

Love,

Shola Adeyemi-Bero,
Attorney at Law

Appendix

Additional information about Mycoplasma pneumonia:

A bacterium called *Mycoplasma pneumonia* called MP. This is the most recognized of all human pathogens. There are over 200 different known species. Most patients with respiratory infection due to *Mycoplasma pneumoniae* don't develop pneumonia. Once inside the body, the bacterium may attach itself to your lung tissue and multiply until a full infection develops. Most cases are mild.

In many healthy adults, the immune system is capable of fighting MP before it can grow into an infection. Those who are most at risk include:

- older adults
- people who have diseases that compromise their immune system, such as HIV
- people who have lung disease
- people who have sickle cell disease
- children younger than age 5

The symptoms of MP are the same as a common upper respiratory tract infection.

Common symptoms of MP include:

- persistent fever
- dry cough
- malaise
- fever

The disease generally develops silently for the first one to three weeks after exposure. Diagnosis is difficult in the early stages because the body doesn't instantly reveal an infection. Sometimes manifestations of infection may occur outside of your lung. If this happens, signs of infection may include the breakup of red blood cells, a skin rash, and joint involvement. The symptoms and signs can indicate infection of the gastrointestinal tract, central nervous system, and heart disease. Three to seven days after the first symptoms appear, medical testing can show evidence of an MP infection.

In order to make a diagnosis, your doctor will listen to your breathing with a stethoscope for any abnormal sounds. A chest X-ray and a CT scan may also help your doctor to make a diagnosis. The first line of treatment for MP is antibiotics. Children get different antibiotics than adults to avoid any potentially dangerous side effects.

Macrolides, the first choice of antibiotics for children, include:
- erythromycin
- clarithromycin
- roxithromycin
- azithromycin

Not all people respond to antibiotic treatment. Alternative treatments include the following corticosteroids: prednisolonemethyl prednisone[11].

Rare Side Effects from the use of Diclofenac:

Symptoms of overdose:
- agitation
- blurred vision
- change in consciousness
- change in the ability to see colors, especially blue or yellow
- confusion
- depression
- difficult or troubled breathing
- hives
- hostility
- irregular, fast or slow, or shallow breathing
- irritability
- loss of consciousness
- muscle twitching
- nervousness

- pain or discomfort in the chest, upper stomach, or throat
- pale or blue lips, fingernails, or skin
- puffiness or swelling of the eyelids or around the eyes, face, lips, or tongue
- rapid weight gain
- seizures
- sleepiness
- slow or fast heartbeat
- stupor
- swelling of the face, ankles, or hands
- tightness in the chest
- trouble sleeping
- unusual drowsiness, dullness, or feeling of sluggishness

I knew that I had to get Olivier off of the medicine and life support. I also knew that he was alive and only sleeping. He was not a vegetable. The Spirit of the Lord revealed to me that once Olivier was off the medication, he would recover fully.

Here are some of the other symptoms of overdose which were very rare yet Olivier experienced:

Nervous system – All of these symptoms occurred in Olivier except for Meningitis although it was suspected.

Common (1% to 10%): Dizziness, headaches
Rare (less than 0.1%): Meningitis
Very rare (less than 0.01%): Memory impairment
Frequency not reported: Confusion, drowsiness, insomnia, paresthesia, tremors

Psychiatric – Oliver had all of the psychiatric symptoms of overdose.

Rare (less than 0.1%): Hallucinations
Very rare (less than 0.01%): Disorientation, depression, nightmare, irritability, psychotic disorder
Frequency not reported: Anxiety, nervousness

Other – He experienced vertigo and persistent fevers though it is unsure whether this was a result of MP or the medication.

Common (1% to 10%): Tinnitus,
Rare (less than 0.1%): Hearing impairment
Frequency not reported: Fever, asthenia, vertigo

Ocular – Olivier had blurred vision, visual disturbance i.e. double vision

Rare (less than 0.1%): Conjunctivitis
Very rare (less than 0.01%): Blurred vision, visual disturbance, diplopia
Frequency not reported: Optic neuritis[12].

References

1. "Product Information. Voltaren (diclofenac)." Novartis Pharmaceuticals, East Hanover, NJ.

2. http://www.webmd.com/

3. https://en.wikipedia.org/wiki/**Opsoclonus_myoclonus**_syndrome

4. http://www.hospitals.sg/hospital/kk-womens-childrens-hospital-kkh

5. http://www.urbandictionary.com/define.php?term=Rhema

6. http://www.sharefaith.com/guide/christian-principles/the-word/rhema-word-of-god.html

7. http://www.drugs.com/keppra.html

8. http://patient.info/health/strong-painkillers-opioids

9. http://www.drugs.com/diclofenac.html

10. http://www.biblewheel.com//Topics/seven.php

11. http://www.healthline.com/health/mycoplasma-pneumonia

12. http://www.drugs.com/sfx/diclofenac-side-effects.html

Note: All quotes taken from the Bible, except otherwise stated, are taken from the New International Version (NIV).

Some names of hospitals and doctors have been changed to protect their identity.

About the Author

Rhonda Wilson-Dikoko was born in Fayette, Alabama on February 3, 1964. Her Father urged her to study nursing after High School so she did. But her real passion was journalism. She dabbled in it during High School and later on took courses in Creative Writing.

Rhonda married Clement Dikoko from Congo, Africa, in 1986 and moved to Congo in 1988. She and her husband, now both ministers, have lived in many different countries doing ministry wherever they go.

They have 3 children Alesea, twins Obiale and Danielle, a son in law Carmelo and two grand-children Olivier and Sanaa. (Family Photo with twins Christmas 2016).

Rhonda has a Devotional on 'Release the Dove' coming out real soon and a few other books to be released at the Lord's bidding.

She and her husband currently reside in The Hague, The Netherlands.

Release the Dove Ministries

© Copyright 2017, Rhonda Wilson-Dikoko

Rhonda Wilson-Dikoko has asserted her right under the Copyright, Designs and Patents Act, 2017, to be identified as Author of this work.

All rights reserved. No part of this publication may be reproduced, stored in a retrieval system, or transmitted, in any form or by any means, electronic, mechanical, photocopying, recording or otherwise, without the prior permission of the publisher or the Copyright Licensing Agency.

Disclaimer: Website references given are correct at time of publication, but may change over time. I cannot guarantee their continued accuracy or availability. This is an actual account of my experience from my point of view. Some names and places may have been changed to protect individuals and institutions.

First Publication January 2017

ISBN-13: 978-1-78222-514-0

www.ingramcontent.com/pod-product-compliance
Lightning Source LLC
Chambersburg PA
CBHW081559040426
42444CB00012B/3166